# THE SOLUTION
## TO
# Peace in the Middle East

By

# Anthony J. Mucciolo

**MUCCIOLO**

**PUBLISHING**
RIDLEY PARK, PA

© All Rights Reserved

© 2011 by Anthony J Mucciolo
Second Edition, 2012

All Scripture verses-unless otherwise indicated-are from the *Holy Bible, King James Version*, KJV® New York: Oxford Edition: 1769. Used by permission. All rights reserved worldwide.

THE HOLY BIBLE, NEW INTERNATIONAL VERSION®, NIV® Copyright © 1973, 1978, 1984, 2011 by Biblica, Inc. ™ Used by permission. All rights reserved worldwide.

All Rights Reserved - No part of this book may be reproduced in any form, by photocopying, or by any electronic or mechanical means, including information storage or retrieval systems, without permission in writing from the copyright owner and the publisher of this book, except by a reviewer who may quote brief passages for promotional purposes in newspapers, periodicals, magazines or journals.

Softcover - 9780985860608

Published by

## MUCCIOLO

## PUBLISHING
Ridley Park, Pa

# DEDICATION

This book is dedicated to the millions of souls who willingly sacrificed their lives, not simply because of their religious "beliefs", but because of their loyalty and esteemed determination to honor the name of their forefather, Abraham, and the *God* he served in righteousness. Their desire and intent to secure the fulfillment of the Covenant *God* made with their father to establish a permanent homeland for his descendants and a Holy Land where the nations could come and worship the Living God was paramount in their hearts.

This book is also dedicated to all Israelis, Palestinians, and Christians inhabiting the land today who share a common heritage and a hope that by the grace of *God*, they will be joined together in a secure bond of peace.

I also want to dedicate this book to my entire family, far and near, all my children and grandchildren, and to all the friends *God* has so graciously given me in this life— both here in America—and in Bethlehem.

Finally, may the Vision and Plan the Lord God of Abraham has predetermined to be enjoyed by *his* seed, be executed in these days for *his* Holy Name's sake, and for the benefit of all the descendants of Abraham.

# ACKNOWLEDGEMENTS

Enough credit cannot be given to the Lord, our Heavenly Father, the Living God, for the inspiration to write this book, for giving me the determination to have it distributed, for the hope that my prayers may be answered, and that the Israelis and Palestinians may reconcile their differences and enjoy the peaceful coexistence they so richly deserve.

Whatever shortcomings there are in this book would have been greatly increased had it not been for my friends, Ishaq Al-Sulaimani, of Philadelphia, Pa. USA; Samuel Akleh, of Bethlehem, Palestine; and Ashraf Zanda, of Jerusalem, who helped me to better understand the many struggles facing the sons of Abraham in Palestine.

I also want to express my sincere gratitude to Barbara Jean Micun for her editing expertise and her creativity in designing the cover for this book.

# TABLE OF CONTENTS

| | |
|---|---|
| Introduction | i |
| Identity Crisis | 1 |
| Foundation–Solid Rock or Sinking Sand | 9 |
| Truth vs. Facts | 15 |
| Questionable Issues | 34 |
| Moses' Encounter with God | 40 |
| God's Blessing to Abraham | 49 |
| The Covenant | 60 |
| Separation of the Sons | 73 |
| Contradiction or Mistranslation | 81 |
| Reconciliation of the Brothers | 87 |
| The Holy Seed | 105 |
| Laying the Groundwork for Peace | 119 |
| Jerusalem | 125 |

# THE SOLUTION

## To

## Peace in the Middle East

# *FOREWORD*

The simplest way to resolve a broken relationship is to take the parties back to the days before their conflicts began. By focusing on a time free of conflict, when love and peace abounded between them, it is much easier to identify the triggers that have resulted in conflict and separation and initiate the potential for a lasting reconciliation.

There is a valid reason why the most resourceful of ambassadors have not been successful in establishing a peace accord acceptable to both parties in a period of more than sixty years. It is no secret the Palestinians have been brushed aside, virtually ignored, and treated as a third world people having little or no education and skill in self governance. Palestinians argue for justice, but their cries fall on deaf ears. Who is listening? And for that matter, who gives any indication they really care? Considering the hostilities they have been subjected to just in the last one hundred years, there is one common denominator that repeatedly presents itself: and based on this perception, it is my contention **the Palestinians are not recognized as a viable identity by the international community, the Israelis, and even several Arab nations.**

History reveals times when the two brothers lived in peace and harmony. Something, or someone, always triggered a conflict to undermine their relationship. We are aware of the origins of the Zionist movement and its impact on the Palestinians, and I don't intend to revisit those events in this book. Nevertheless, from the time Isaac and Ishmael were children, a conspiracy was put into effect that, from my perspective, has triggered every conflict they have had. Furthermore, these triggers are engaged at will by those who expect to profit from their conflict. Besides, what has the rehashing of injurious events accomplished over the past sixty years or more? Have these *negotiations* resulted in an authentic peace accord? No, and they never will. The international community, in feigned attempts to broker a peace agreement, recognizes the Palestinian identity with lip service and promises that were never intended to be fulfilled. They dole out money to "keep them calm"; like giving a cracker to a parrot. I am disturbed writing this, so I can imagine the frustration the reader has reading it.

Palestinian Prime Minister Salam Fayyad expressed the sentiments of the Palestinian people when he said, "I do not know of a single Israeli politician from any party who I would expect to offer a reasonable solution to the Israeli-Palestinian conflict. All of them want a partial solution, or they aim to improve the face and the conditions of the occupation while the settlements continue." **(Haaretz.com Staff and News Agencies - Pub. 07.02.09)**

What do I hope to accomplish that hasn't already been tried? First of all, I intend to reveal the conspiracy and the subconscious triggers that, when pulled, produces an immediate irate reaction from the sons of Ishmael. Secondly, this conspiracy has been draped in a camouflage of deception, lies, and half-truths, which must be unveiled in order for the triggers to be exposed. This can only be accomplished by Truth. Once these triggers are uncovered, the ability to cause further destruction can be virtually eliminated because we are dealing with *pain*, not *craziness*.

Consider the emotional trauma invading every cell in his body, when Ishmael was being sent away from his father's house. I can see a sixteen year old boy begging his father with tears not to send him and his mother away. I can relate to his anger towards Sarah, her rejection of him, and her unjust decision of denying him any inheritance in his father's estate. The more he thought about the conspiracy to ban him from the family of Abraham, the false charges levied against him, and his perception of his father's failure to resist the demands of his wife – to take up his cause against her unjust decision. How could he understand what was happening to him? Without warning, he was being sent away from his father's house and land. He and his father had a very close and loving relationship, yet suddenly his cries and pleadings were totally disregarded. He and his mother had to leave; the decision was final. In his heart, he was alone. Did anyone care about him, and his mother's welfare, safety, or where they would live? In the mind of a sixteen year old, he was unwanted, unloved, thrust into a world of fear and uncertainty. Besides, his teary-eyed father, the last vision he probably had was that of the little brother he loved, who was undoubtedly crying his eyes out at his brother's departure. These were extremely painful and traumatic memories that were rehearsed over and over again to anyone who would listen. He needed to hear a compassionate voice and the extension of someone's hand to feel that he was wanted. He tried to drown these mental images from his mind as the years went by. He had to be a man, now. He had responsibilities, and undoubtedly was advised to put it all behind him and look forward to the future. Interestingly, if we were to focus on the history of

Ishmael and his family, these events were replayed many times over the centuries. The latest repeat began with the founding of the Zionist movement, in the early part of the twentieth century.

I assert that the pain inflicted upon the seed of Ishmael from generations past, and to Isaac as well, has triggered their conflicts, reshaped their identities, deprived them of the unity they were predestined to enjoy, and has always resulted in Ishmael recalling the events and visions that took place on that horrible day; a teary-eyed father, a crying brother, and the denial of his rights as a son of Abraham. They have become such sensitive issues that we can probably call them "hair triggers" because it takes very little stimulus to cause an explosive response.

All of us have experienced one or more hurtful events in our lives that we "believe" we have put behind us because they rarely, if ever come to mind; and perhaps because we feel that we have forgiven those who hurt us. However, some years later someone will do or say something that triggers what may be an aggressive or excessively emotional outburst, as our subconscious mind braces to endure the pain we suffered many years before. Our reactions are often surprising, even to ourselves; and if we begin to have multiple explosive outbursts of anger, rage, or physical confrontation, we begin to develop a reputation, a new identity, in the minds of others. Oftentimes, without proper diagnosis, these outbursts are attributed to hormonal changes, depression, or other "mental deficiencies." Instead of searching for the root cause, the triggers, that amplify and expose our "anger issues" as some might call them, we find ourselves being prescribed some pills to calm us down. Does this act, in any way, correct the way people see us? We are no longer recognized as we once were; we are the emotional, untrustworthy, mental cases – so it is enough just to simply give the parrot a cracker and shut him up.

In order for Ishmael's descendants to gain respect from the international community, have their cries for justice heard instead of ignored, and change their identity from crazed extremists to the loving, just, and charitable seed of Abraham, I must take them back to the days before they left Abraham's camp, unfortunately revisit the trauma, and successfully argue for their right to Abraham's estate. The Covenant of Abraham will supply the proofs I need to substantiate my conclusions.

My intended audiences are the Palestinians, Israelis, and Palestinian Christians, whom I hope will find illumination, re-establish their true identities as the children of Abraham, and use the suggestions and guidelines in this book to begin a permanent reconciliation. **I intend to prove that Ishmael was denied the right to claim his inheritance rights in Canaan; and that their problems today are a direct result of these schemes and the suffering they caused.**

The identity and recognition of the Palestinians and Arabs who claim their descendency from Abraham must be authenticated. That which is authentic must have all misconceptions and inconsistencies, both in context and perception, resolved according to the edicts of truth, not opinions and beliefs.

Discovering truth is a slow process. It is not merely repeating the words of a prophet, or holy book. Truth is found after all the residue, the conflicts, inconsistencies and ambiguities are removed. To begin with, everyone should be completely aware of what I call truth, how I have come to identify it, the work truth engages in, and how Truth fulfills its work. If I don't spend time on this subject, then everyone will be left with another "opinion," and this book will join many others gathering dust on the shelves marked, "Opinions and Ideas."

There are Facts; and there are Truths. There are perceptions, opinions, ideas and hypothethicals. But, I am firmly convinced the Israeli-Palestinian conflict will never be resolved on the basis of anything but the absolute truth; and truth doesn't accomplish its goals by bringing up old dirt. Truth causes the tender stem of a new plant to break through the coldest and most impregnable dirt. This is the plan, the decree, and the work *God* is about to perform in the lives of the Palestinians. For our Heavenly Father, the *God* of Abraham, has heard your groans, seen your miseries, and has determined to lift from your shoulders the yoke of affliction.

I am inclined to believe the question of Ishmael's entitlement was raised during the leadership of Joshua as he began to divide the land between the twelve families of Israel. If so, the issue would have been brought to the judges, who were probably unable to validate the Covenant made between *God* and Abraham, and turned to the priests to resolve the question. I can't imagine any other way that a "legal question" became a religious debate separating the brothers.

The Israelis have been successful in gaining recognition as a people and as a country on the international front. They believe they are entitled to do as they wish on *their land* because Israel has been recognized as the legitimate homeland of the Jews. They have been identified by many Christian denominations as the *Chosen people of God* as well. **That is their identity**; and one that is **supported by governments and religions. What is the proper identity of the Palestinians?**

A valid declaration or decree as to who is rightfully entitled to the land of Canaan is essential before there will ever be a lasting peace in the land. It is not enough to sit at the table and quote the Torah or Qur'an because as the last fifteen hundred years has shown, that practice has not succeeded in establishing peace. We have spent too many years rehashing the age-old histories of "He did!" "They did!" This is the result, not the cause, of the animosity, antagonism, and hostile actions perpetrated by one brother against the other.

The reality is this—if it can be proven that Israel is the only one rightfully entitled to the land, then they will have an identity and recognition that would forever quash any future claims by the Palestinians. The same is true for the Palestinians should it be determined they are the rightful heirs. But what if it could be proven they are both equally entitled to the land according to the Covenant *God* made with Abraham?

## *GOD'S WORD?*

Any writer who declares his narrative contains the inspired Word of *God*, and *his* will, must also be able to reveal *God's* magnificent wisdom. *The Solution* does exactly that. I can say with unashamed meekness the foundation for a lasting peace revealed in this book never once entered my mind. I never imagined a resolution that would not require the Palestinians and Israelis to surrender one square inch of the land. Secondly, an idea that would eliminate the possibility of dividing the Holy City of Jerusalem was far beyond anything I could contrive. Everyone will be able to bear witness to the Lord's wisdom as he makes known *his* desire for Jerusalem; and I can assure the Israelis and Palestinians they will not be disappointed.

I am aware of some of the theological differences between the Jewish and Muslim religions, though I must admit that I am not as familiar with the Qur'an as I am with the Hebrew and Christian Bibles I have studied at length. My reading and study of the Qur'an is not adequate for me to examine, comment on, or to use in this writing with any degree of accuracy or consistency. Let no one think that I have purposely distanced myself from the Qur'an, or that I am trying to promote the Bible with subtlety. Such a statement would be completely false. It is out of respect for the Qur'an and Islam, that I limit the possibilities of misstating or mistranslating verses that could potentially cast a shadow upon their merits. Otherwise, this writing would be more susceptible to debate and rejection than as a document that offers hope and a solution to the conflict at hand. I beg the indulgence of the Islamic clergy for my lack of expertise required to examine the Qur'an's writings in the same manner as I will be examining the Hebrew Scriptures. I hope to advance my learning in the Qur'an in the future, but the situation that engulfs the Israeli and Palestinians' lives today warrants that I bring forth this writing without further delay.

Let me also state for the record that I have no intention of promoting *believed*, *revealed*, or *contrived* religious theories *using* scriptural and prophetic references to back up my <u>*opinions*</u>. I find this method of advancing "truth" immoral and reprehensible. Nor is it my intent to *name and blame*. My objective is to examine the Covenant between *God* and Abraham, identify the heir(s), and articulate its provisions.

I consider it a grave matter, worthy of the most woeful consequences, when someone declares they have received a message from *God*, or had some "truth" revealed to them by Divine inspiration, when it is obvious they are unable to identify the essence and character of *truth*. To make a statement asserting that *God* gave a message that a mortal man would be able to easily contradict or dismiss as an empty opinion, *to me*, is blasphemous. Therefore, I will compose a narrative describing *truth* as I have come to recognize it; and the method I have learned and practice that enables me to separate truths from assumed *opinion*s, *facts*, and *beliefs* in circulation today, and to present my findings to the interested parties.

In a world corrupted by individuals claiming to possess and preach the <u>Truth</u>, I feel compelled to validate the arguments and conclusions presented here as—*the Lord's Solution*—not mine, one that has the likelihood of bringing peace to Palestinians and Israelis alike if adopted. I hope that my arguments will convince all Arabs and Israelis to revisit <u>*the Covenant*</u> in the light of it being the Will and Testament of *God* and their father, Abraham; examine the wording, affirm its intent, ratify its contents, and expedite its execution.

## *IDENTITY CRISIS*

I travelled to Palestine in January 2008, spending six days in the West Bank among some of the most beautiful people I have ever met in my life. For some unexplainable reason I was drawn to Bethlehem; I visited the city three times in that week: I felt at home, like I belonged there.

I went; I saw; and I was sickened by the oppressive state of affairs. I remember returning to my hotel room the first night absorbed with the visions of hopelessness and depression on the faces of many Palestinians I witnessed in my travels in the West Bank. I turned my attention to the Lord and asked, "Holy Father, is there no solution to their problem?" It was there I saw the root cause of the problems affecting Israelis and Palestinians and received the message I have written here.

What comes to mind when we hear one of the following words: Palestinians, Hamas, Hezbollah, Iranian, Koreans, or Pakistanis? Each one carries its own identity, its own reputation, does it not?

What is the general perception of the Palestinians? How does it contrast with that of the Israelis? Prior to the advent of the Zionists, the accounts of the daily lives of the Palestinians typically supports the position they lived quietly and modestly, purposely separating themselves and their children from the temptations and evils of an immoral society; and were seemingly quite content to live a life unencumbered by the allure of riches and power. They submitted to the authority of the Islamic clergy and gave themselves to daily prayer, giving thanks to *God* for providing their essential needs. Who can find fault with people who desire to live a life pleasing to *God?*

However, to their surprise, their lives would suddenly change. They were about to relive a day in their history, one they have witnessed more than once. Their land was occupied by Great Britain, whose ministry proceeded to divide the *land of Palestine* into parcels; Jewish sections, Arab sectors, British controlled areas, including Jerusalem; which **they declared** was to remain an international city for people of all faiths. The Palestinians protested as the British systematically stripped the land of their fathers from them; they cried out for justice, to no avail. Were there Jews living along side of them who were also protesting the injustices being imposed on their friends? Yes, but, like Isaac, their cries were ignored as well.

One unknown secular Jew, Theodor Herzl, began what came to be known as the Zionist movement. *He* **decided, without any consultation with the Palestinians,** to make Palestine the permanent homeland for the *Jews,* convincing the English the land was barren and unoccupied. Sir Arthur Balfour, of the British foreign ministry made the following declaration, **"His majesty's government views with favor the establishment in Palestine of a national home for the Jewish people."**

From the mouth of the Palestinians to my ears, I could imagine the screams and the expressions of shock and exasperation:

- Who are **they to take control of our nation**?
- **They** do not own the land: they have no claims here; so by what authority are **they** empowered to decide who will inhabit it and where they will be permitted to reside?
- What do **they** make themselves; and what powers do **they** possess over us that permits **them** to impose **their** decisions on us?
- Who are they to decide that Jerusalem will be an international city?

If I were arguing on behalf of the Palestinians, as one oblivious to any "triggers" being set off; I would demand to know what right the United Nations or any other government entity has to enter upon my land and dictate the terms **we must agree to**, in order for us **to remain on our own land**. I would be enraged and undoubtedly provoked to violence as I witnessed them giving away our land to the Zionists! Would my actions provoke the British or the Zionists to identify me as a maniac or a lunatic? Would I care? No!

I can just imagine how we Americans would react if we were occupied by a foreign nation and given a U.N. dictate to vacate our homes and land. Then, to add insult to injury, **they** decide to "**give our land**" to someone else! I think we would do what the French, Polish, Hungarians, and other nations did when the Germans occupied their countries. They formed militias to drive the Germans off their land. The Allies supported their "resistance" because it benefitted them. We would do the same thing if our military was incapable of stopping **their** invasion. Did the

West label the French, Poles, and Hungarians, as terrorists? Would they call us terrorists if we had to form our own militias to fight off an invading army? If so, maybe we should simply label every human being a terrorist, because we would all do the same things! I cannot think of any nation, occupied by a foreign army, who would not resist. By the way, the French, Polish, etc. were not labeled terrorists. They were **The Resistance**! When I fought in Viet Nam in 1966-67, the Vietnamese **Resistance** were labeled **Viet Cong** and **Guerrillas**! I suppose they saved the word, **Terrorists**, for the Palestinians and Muslims. Is there a difference between the tactics of one "terror group" and another? Now that I have repeated some of the allegations against the Israelis and Palestinians, what good thing can we expect to come out of this? It raises our anger, our blood pressure, and accomplishes nothing but frustration.

I am not supporting violence and terrorism. I have seen first-hand the evils of terrorism. These acts are nauseating; and will never result in peace. Peace-loving Palestinians, out of necessity, must distinguish themselves from those who promote terror. Palestinian *Extremists* have made it a practice of carrying out attacks against vulnerable women and children of the *Occupation*. As a result, they have hurt their own people more than they have the Israelis, because their actions have distorted the credibility and integrity of their Palestinian identity, and have given the media and their propagandists' reason to blaspheme the Qur'an, the Arab people, and their religion.

*Palestinians must come to the realization their status in the Middle East has been compromised, even among neighboring Arab states. Their identity has been blemished, distorted, and impossible to define with any degree of integrity. This is a major dilemma, a major cause of their frustrations and failures to advance their agenda; and it must be resolved.*

The international community cannot, (will not) accept the Arab and Palestinian positions based on a religious argument. Neither will they entertain an argument on the premise of adverse possession. A claim for right of possession, especially if based on entitlements named in an inheritance dispute, must be challenged in a "legal" setting with the claimant presenting viable evidence.

It is a common belief, especially among many Christians I have conversed with, that Israel is behind these attitudes and behaviors toward the seed of Ishmael and, "they have a right to!" For many, it is their *belief* that when Abraham sent Ishmael away, he stripped him of all inheritance rights in accordance with Sarah's demands. Consequently, Israel rejected the Palestinians' claims of entitlement and contended that if they remained in the land, the Palestinians should submit to Israeli government rule or, be removed from the land. Those are very strong *beliefs*! Has it been absolutely "proven" these *beliefs* are grounded in truth? No. they have not.

There are parties who, in their ignorance, are encouraging a major outbreak between the Palestinians, Israelis, and Arabs. For one, the *international community* is increasing the pressure on them to establish a peace accord under its terms. This pressure will ultimately force the parties into a position where all negotiations will reach a hopeless impasse and result in a needless war. Then again, we also have the Armageddon prophets who truly "believe" this final war is predetermined by *God* and must take place in order to usher in the Messianic kingdom on earth. I'm not arguing against the prophecy, for it will be fulfilled; however, there is some confusion over who the contenders are in this final war—*another identity problem*.

I've been searching the Scriptures for years trying to find where it was written the last battle will be fought between Ishmael and Isaac. The only prophecies I have come across indicate the combatants in this war will be those who *oppose the righteous precepts of God* versus *those who embrace them*—the wicked sinners versus Abraham's children—not Isaac versus Ishmael. I am confident the wicked desperately want to see a major war break out between the two brothers, as it would serve their purposes well. Since many Christians are likely to stand with Israel, the numbers of "believers" who acknowledge and try to follow the precepts ordained by *God* would be decimated to the point that wickedness would have a clear path to world domination. Amazingly, it is believed this concept is within the scope of *God's* will. Once again, we can see evidence of another *misidentification problem*. However, I can say with absolute confidence that the perfect will of *God*, *at this time*, is to provide a <u>Solution</u> to the hostilities between Abraham's seed; a *judicious solution* to the conflict that *God* foreknew would arise between *his* children; a <u>Solution</u> that will not establish one a *Winner* and the other a *Loser*; as neither party will *he* deem to be Right, and the other

Wrong. However, make no mistake about it, if this _Solution_ is not acceptable, or if the parties cannot find a better one to replace it, a tragic war is inevitable. The authorities in high places are determined to eradicate Israel, the Palestinians, and the Christians. Unless the descendants of Abraham keep this in mind, the days of murder and atrocities will come upon us like a thief breaking into our homes in the night when we are the most vulnerable. If you search the Scriptures, you will find many prophecies in this regard.

**This is the issue I am devoting this book to—presenting viable evidence to substantiate the Palestinians' standing, identity, and their inalienable right of possession.**

I am hopeful that my efforts will relieve the living conditions and lessen the suffering of the Palestinians. If I am successful, the Israelis will also benefit immensely. I intend to take us back in history, before Ishmael's exile, to the time the Covenant was created between _God_ and Abraham. I will examine, unravel, and unveil the _truths contained in the Covenant of Promise_—particularly those irrefutable exposés that depict the true intentions of the parties involved. Contrary to some religious beliefs, I will **prove** whether Ishmael is entitled to all the rights, privileges, and advantages the Israelis enjoy. This is not an indictment of the Israelis, Christians, or their faiths. According to Moses, _God_ made the Covenant with Abraham. If this statement is valid, the Wisdom of _God_ should be present, and _he_ will bear witness to the rightful heir(s). I will reveal more on this statement a little later in this book.

It is certainly within the parameters of God's Divine grace and wisdom that if Ishmael can be positively identified as a joint heir with Isaac, that both brothers come out winners. Assuming Ishmael's inclusion as an heir of Abraham and of the Holy Land, the proof that *his* wisdom is present in the writing of this book will manifest itself in the following ways: First, Israelis and Palestinians will not **"have to surrender"** one inch of land to the other. Secondly, they will not **"have to divide"** the Holy City of Jerusalem, nor will they permit it to become an international city governed by foreign nations. Thirdly, **the issue of who is rightfully entitled to the land will be resolved** in accordance with the Covenant *God* made with Abraham and his seed **for their own peace and safety,** not for the economic stability or advantage of any other nation. If the Palestinians are rightfully entitled to make a claim, this book will bear this out. Afterwards, either peace will triumph without war; or there will be a war of decimation.

Here is a thought to meditate upon, **Truth is capable of revealing, and then removing, "invisible walls" that prevent *God's* people from moving forward.**

## _FOUNDATION—Solid Rock or Sinking Sand_

Reconciling a broken relationship is a difficult and tedious work of love. Trying to reconcile a relationship where one does not recognize the other is even more difficult. If Israel, or Ishmael, conducts himself as though he cannot "recognize" his brother, reconciliation will be a nearly impossible task. At the same time, it is also safe to say that without a willingness to resolve the differences, the parties would never reconcile whether they acknowledge each other's identities or not.

Recognition precedes a welcome. If a person is seen as friendly, he can be welcomed into one's home. However, if he is perceived to be dishonest, or to have mischief in his heart, he will not be welcome. Recognizing the approach of an individual that has hurt us is often met with immediate rejection or a high degree of suspicion. This is why **Identity** coupled with a **Welcome** is the first step in the process of **Reconciliation**.

Peace without reconciliation is merely a truce. Both parties have brokered many truces, but have never reconciled their differences. Palestinians want Israel and the world to perceive them as a people of integrity who are desirous of a lasting peace and willing to pave a path to reconciliation and tranquility. In short, the mediator must be able to convince the Israelis there are emotional triggers at the heart of the conflict; triggers the Israelis and their allies are setting off, perhaps unknowingly.

I will devote more time to this discussion a little later; but I will insert this statement here: the first work of *Truth* is reconciliation. **Hope is the solid foundation upon which truth is established,** the minimal amount of faith needed for truth to begin its work, and sets the stage for a possible resolution. However, in order for true peace and reconciliation to take place *truth* **must engage and overcome one of its greatest enemies, the <u>adversary of truth</u>, which disguises itself as "faith" and deceives many.** If hope is the foundation of truth, then the adversary of hope, the spirit of mistrust and suspicion, will try to replace its rock-solid foundation with a foundation built on sand to limit the chances of reconciliation and build upon past hurts to provoke doubt, dissention, controversy, and ill will.

Who can successfully mediate a relationship broken by disappointments, rejection and abandonment, deceptions, deprivation, lies, and emotional, mental, and physical pain? *Truth* **is the only mediator** that can succeed in prevailing over these bitter emotions, assuage the deep rooted anger associated with them, and begin to nurture a slow healing process.

Another enemy of "true faith" is publicized and widely known as the doctrine of *acceptance by faith*, particularly in religious circles. Many religious bodies require the "congregate" to accept the doctrines and claims of their religion and its leadership without question or doubt. Just imagine how simple life would be if we accepted everything we can't see by faith! For example, the first established religion would still be in practice today without any competition if everyone simply *accepted by faith* those doctrines that were widely believed five thousand years ago! This type of "faith" is divisive; it never reconciles, and is never a convincing negotiator for opposing views. While religions may successfully promote this view and defend itself against a "heretic's challenge", *God's* law and civil law is not afforded such latitude. Civil law demands the critical examination of all written and oral testimony presented by a witness. Without sustainable proofs one's testimony is valid, injustices would flourish.

The Palestinians languish over the injustices imposed upon them by individuals who accept the propaganda and misinformation they hear without questioning its validity. Consequently, their outcries of *injustice* fall on deaf ears. This doctrine of *acceptance by faith* has succeeded in marring their image, integrity, religion, and respectability by virtue of malicious reporting and distorted information. I will present another illustration, a parable of sorts.

A judge is presented a copy of a will that clearly identifies the parties, their relationship, a clear description of the real and personal property to be transferred, and a statement declaring that his entire estate would pass to his sons. Standing before the court, one of the sons asserts that he is the "sole and rightful heir" designated in the will that the statements therein are ambiguous and his estranged brother has difficulty understanding them. He further testifies that his father sent his brother away and that he was "disinherited" by his family. The judge listens to the arguments and, without requiring any additional evidence, makes a decision based on "blind faith" that the *petitioner's* *testimony* is much more credible and awards him the estate. The son, victimized by the judge, is filled with rage and vows to continue his quest to claim what is rightfully his, even if that means he must resort to violence and war. As the years go by, certain *prophets* arise who claim to have had a vision in which the *Divine Messenger* appeared to them and revealed that the victimized son was the sole and rightful heir entitled to claim his father's estate. These so-called *enlightened ones, "false* prophets"*, were believable and elevated to prominent positions over the flock.

So, how do we know they were false prophets? A "true prophet" would have tried to reconcile the conflict. He would have delivered a message of truth similar to this one to **all** the children of Abraham: "Our people received a verdict from an unrighteous judge who *accepted by faith* an argument for which he should have demanded more evidence before making a decision. Then, we added to his error by also *accepting by faith* the words of "prophets" without seeking confirmation *God* sent them. Therefore, **we must accept responsibility for our own decisions and actions that brought suffering and death to our father, Abraham's seed.**" According to the *Godly* prophet, everyone had a part in the wrongdoing. He proceeded to project the virtues of Truth in accordance with God's word, "There is none righteous; no, not one." Then, as was common practice for a prophet of *God*, he would have called for a day of prayer, repentance, and sacrificial offerings, to seek the forgiveness of *God* for the blood they shed in ignorance. Then he would have sought the wisdom of *God* to reconcile the brothers. This is *God's* way.

Now, if we tried to justify our position and insist on laying blame on one of the parties, which one would we choose - the judge, or one of the sons. How would we make the determination? Unless we do the proper thing and demand some verifiable proof, we would be adding to the judge's error by *accepting his decision by faith*. **Truth is not determined by who makes the stronger argument!**

It is my understanding that Jews and Muslims claim to have accepted the Covenant by faith and do not require any validation of its authenticity; and furthermore, it is their position their ancestors and the prophets legitimized the Covenant, and the notion of scrutinizing it for any inconsistencies is completely unwarranted. For many, the idea of questioning the sanctity or legality of the Covenant, much less examining it for discrepancies, is a grave matter bordering on heresy and blasphemy.

However, to demean or denigrate the sacredness of the Scriptures is not in my heart at all. I contend that someone, a judge, elder, prophet, or sage, presented this same issue before the elders, most likely nearing the end of Moses' life, and/or the beginning of Joshua's leadership; and, an unfair decision was made based on their religious "beliefs", personal bias, or peer pressure. Who it was, and the reasons given, are not available to us, but the reality of the unjust decision and the conflict that resulted from his decision is still affecting us today. Ishmael apparently was denied a portion among his brothers in the land of Canaan. Was the decision a fair one, a correct one? Were Ishmael's descendants "recognized" as joint heirs? Or, were they given the identity of an "estranged brother" or some other designation? Once again, they set off the triggers that aroused the Ishmaelites' anger, even the same ones affecting them today. These "judges" provoked hostile feelings and created a situation that would ultimately require the intercession of *God's* work of Reconciliation to restore their relationship. Of course, I will present enough substance to validate my assertion.

A detailed account of the Covenant of Promise is available to us in the Torah and Christian Scriptures. The Qur'an acknowledges the Covenant but with less specificity. My focus will be on the language, content, and structure of Abraham's Covenant as I search for distinguishing characteristics typically found in a testator's final will and testament. If I find evidence to support this position, then essentially I will treat it *as a legal document and base my examination on this premise.* Why? Because a Will and Testament is only probated based on its contents, and the factual evidence presented, not one's religious or personal beliefs.

When arguing religious and political positions, the parties ultimately agree on two points: first, they agree that they disagree; and secondly, they concede that it is virtually impossible to convince the other side their position is the right one— if a "right one" even exists.

**I contend that <u>this conflict is, and will forever be, a civil matter—not a religious one, which I intend to prove.</u>**

## *TRUTH vs. FACTS*

My questions and arguments may provoke some sensitive and uncomfortable emotions, but once again, be assured it is not my intention, desire, or quest to disparage anyone's religion or their Holy Scriptures. Neither is it my position to support one over the other. However, before I continue with this work, I feel compelled to depart from the main subject and give time to a topic of great importance, ***the character and nature of truth versus stated facts.***

It is a "fact" that Ishmael and his mother were sent away from Abraham's camp because Sarah decided that Ishmael would not share in the inheritance with Isaac. But, facts never reveal hidden truths. Palestinians have questions that require answers. "Is this the whole truth?" "Was it Abraham's intent to disinherit Ishmael?" "Was it the will of *God* that he be dispossessed and cut-off from his father's house?" Can these questions be answered in truth? They must be, out of necessity.

If the Israelis and Palestinians were able to differentiate between truth, opinion, and *beliefs*, my question is, "Why hasn't this issue been resolved long before now?" Who stands to profit from their conflict in the religious communities? I can understand why entities that provide weapons would want to keep the hostilities ongoing; but religions and clergymen, who must give an answer to *God* for their actions? No, I can't understand their reasoning, if it even exists among them. I prefer to believe they would encourage peace rather than slaughter.

Nevertheless, I feel that it is imperative that I give this dissertation on *truth*. The land in dispute, the land of Canaan, was included in the Covenant made between *God*, Abraham, and his seed. The Palestinians have been denied any claim to inheritance. They are maligned and their cries are ignored; but to substantiate the truth, it must first be identified. Before agreeing to another peace accord "doomed to failure" the Israelis and Palestinians should be certain the terms regarding *"rightful entitlement," "dividing the land into two states,"* or *"dividing Jerusalem,"* coincide with the original intent of the parties named in the Covenant. Abraham has gone to his place of rest; but the Lord, the *God* of Abraham, is still very much alive; and I don't think it would be wise to amend an agreement that *he* was a party to, without convincing assurance that *he* was in complete accord. For this reason, I must be absolutely certain the arguments I make in this book successfully reveal its truths; otherwise, they will have no value.

My representations of truth are indigenous to this book, and should be important to everyone. I am certain that over a period of six decades the Israelis and Palestinians have endured "talks" that presented a great number of creative opinions; and I seriously doubt they are desirous of another one. Besides, I am a firm believer that no one should ever *accept by faith* another's declaration of *truth* without requiring the individual to describe how he arrived at his conclusions, the process he used to validate them, and more importantly, to describe the nature and character of the *God* he believes in; because *truth* is only revealed by *God*. To simply say something like, "The Bible says," is insufficient. Satan can quote more Bible verses (his iron swords) faster than any believer I've ever met.

This is a grave matter; one we should all be aware of. Everyone, whether they realize it or not, (and I certainly was unaware) is given the choice of which tree we will eat from, the tree of life, or the tree of knowledge. Unknowingly, we all face the same dilemma Adam was challenged with in the Garden of Eden.

Adam decided to risk his eternal life, put his soul on the gambling table set before him, and make his wager, (I'm speaking figuratively). What was he gambling on? The stakes were high; and in order to *win*, he had to wager all that he had, his **life**, on what he *believed to be the truth*. What were his choices? He could *believe the words of his wife (or the serpent) that he would become like a god;* or, he could *believe the words of God that he was ordained to rule over all the earth*. In addition, part of the wager included a provision that he reject *God's* word that *he would die if he ate of the tree of knowledge*. Was he forced to gamble? No; he only needed to call out to the Living God and ask *him* to validate the truth. We all know the story: he decided to gamble his life on what he *chose to believe* and lost.

This is the reality each of us are faced with—**gamble our eternal life on what we *choose to believe,* or what we *choose to disbelieve*; or we can *choose to call on the Lord*** and ask him to reveal *his* truth. *God* forbid that I should be found guilty of putting a soul at risk of spending an eternity in utter darkness! How would I defend myself on Judgment Day if I was accused of denying one his eternal salvation by asking him or her to accept *my opinions* or *beliefs* as the truth? I couldn't.

One who claims to have had the truth revealed to him should have a personal testimony of the character and nature of his *God* and be able to declare the truths *God revealed about Himself.* Take notice that I said—about *Himself!* If I can't identify with his voice, or manner of speaking, how can I be certain of the speaker's identity? If I profess that the *God* I believe in is merciful and gracious, am I quoting Scriptures I have learned and *choose to believe*; or am I a true witness? A true witness is able to verify the rationale behind his claims by testifying of his personal experiences. However, let me be clear about one thing; all experiences and testimonies must be in agreement with those of the apostles and prophets of old, and void of all contradictions and inconsistencies.

*Truth* has become synonymous with *logical reason, eyewitness account, stated facts, prophetic utterances,* and *long-established hypotheses,* to name but a few. In many religious circles, the *truth* is confined to one definition, description, classification, and source; and often includes a doctrine that truth is only revealed to certain enlightened ones chosen to receive divine revelation. On the basis of these arguments, they contend their teachings should not be subjected to a barrage of simple questions, but the faithful should simply *"accept them by faith."* However persuasive the argument may be, it is void of *truth*; as it only serves to enable these "leaders" to manage what is believed, and to exercise rule over their congregations.

What is *truth*? I will begin to answer this question by disclosing my own personal testimony, and how I began my search. During my first experience I was made to realize that I did not **know** what the truth was; that what I believed—my faith, and spiritual education—was the by-product of many years of accepting opinions and ideas as truths. But when it was made real to me that I was gambling my eternal soul on what I *believed* to be true, my heart was filled with a fear that remains with me to this day. I was only aware of what my religion taught, and I also knew I had doubts about the faith since I was a child.

On that first day, I turned my eyes toward the sky and reached out to *God*. "I don't know what the truth is," I began. "I don't know if what I was taught is true or not. I mean, how do I know that Jesus wasn't a 'Superman' type hero of his day, and what is taught about him was written to entertain wild-eyed children? How do I know the Jews are not right—that Jesus was merely a prophet? As of right now, Lord, I am setting aside everything I have ever heard or learned about *you*: I don't believe anything anymore. I don't know *your* name, and I don't even know if *you* are real, if *you* really exist, or not; but if *you* do, and there is a Day of Judgment, I don't want to stand before *you* on that day and hear *you* ask me, 'Why did you put your trust in some idiot that didn't know what he was talking about? Why didn't you ask *me*?' No, Lord; from this day forth, I will be asking *you* to reveal *your* truth to me; and if *you* don't reveal *yourself* and *your* word, then I won't believe anything." Afterwards, I began to question the sanity of my prayer, but fortunately, *he* didn't let me give up on my request. It became my fervent prayer that *God* would reveal *himself* to me, (if *he* was a living being); and that if *he* did not, I would adopt the atheistic view that simple minded, uneducated men *created* gods to explain those things they could not understand. I prayed that *he* would allow me to **know** *him*, to **know** *he* was a living persona, to **know** *his* name, to **know** if *he* was capable of being sensitive to the concerns and fears of us lowly humans. I wanted to know the truth about Jesus. My questions were endless, but I can testify that I was never disappointed; in fact, I was pleasantly surprised that *he* was content to answer them all.

I am intensely grateful to the Lord for this experience because it turned out to be the beginning of my successful search for truth. And, I can say with all honesty that if *he* had not revealed *himself* to me, there is no way that I would be a believer in *him* today. Over the last thirty five years of continual instruction, *he* taught me how to separate ideas and opinions from truth. I was repeatedly reminded to pay close attention to one's words, ask the speaker what he meant if he used words that had multiple meanings, and (admittedly the toughest discipline to master) **never begin to think of what you're going to say until the last word is spoken!** The most significant of truths I had to discover was that I needed to have my ears in a perpetual state of alert, to be vigilant, constantly aware that *his* words of **truth, life, wisdom, righteousness faith, light, and love,** *the most identifiable characteristics of the true God*, the keys of salvation and deliverance that can unlock the gates of Hell, open every prison door, and deliver the prisoners held captive. The challenges are usually difficult, but the victories are sweet.

I was taught that if I were to study a topic simply to gather information in order to engage in a debate with someone else; I would never find truth. I would only be successful in finding truth if I concentrated on listening for, and confirming, that the person and essential qualities of *God* were present. This was how I came to identify the incredible virtues of Almighty *God* and *his* will—who nurtures us with an incredible love that overcomes our fears—and gives us *his* peace, mercy, grace, forgiveness, and so much more. *He* opened my eyes to *his* righteousness and showed me the power of *his* truth—a truth that draws all mankind to *him* and makes it impossible not to fall in love with *him* as we come to **know** *him*.

The qualitative essence of truth can be likened to the characteristics of light. Light rays are invisible to the naked eye; yet, they have perceptible features that enable us to discern, identify, and definitively confirm their reality, power (energy), and benefits. And, like the rays emanating from the sun, it is impossible for the earth to fully absorb, to the exclusion of all other heavenly bodies, the massive volume of energy and light it produces. Similarly, it isn't possible for one human being or religious group to absorb the fullness of "truth" to the exclusion of all others.

The concept that truth is invisible to the naked eye defies some rational thought, but so does the assertion that truth has the attributes of a living personality, such as *God*. This was a concept endorsed by Jesus of Nazareth and his disciples. How did they substantiate this "belief"? They expanded the characteristics of *truth* by alleging that the essence of *truth* is much more profound than simple words:

that it actually possesses an invisible living persona, a conscious nature. This idea was completely alien to me; and since I had never heard this before, I was full of questions.

Let me include this statement for anyone and everyone who desires to seek truth. **God is fully accessible to all who seek *him*. I am no more privileged than any other. Furthermore, there is no question *he* will refuse to answer, as long as your purpose is to search for truth, not to debate someone you don't agree with.**

An early Church father wrote: ***"...And it is the Spirit that beareth witness, because <u>the Spirit is truth.</u>*** (1 John 5.6 *emphasis added*) He referred to *truth* as a *Living Spirit* capable of <u>testifying.</u> Is the Spirit a suitable witness? An authentic witness is described as an individual who demonstrates his capacity to rationalize, remember critical details, recall information from memory; and then testify to its certainty. His statements are examined and every attempt is made to reveal any inaccuracies or inconsistencies: if none are found, his testimony will be considered credible. If this definition is factually correct: before we can confirm John's statement that "the *Spirit* is truth: we must be able to conclude the Spirit is a *Persona* capable of reasoning and giving a valid testimony. You will witness one of the ways this is done later in this book.

Jesus of Nazareth, as reported in the Christian New Testament, a preacher familiar to most Jews and Muslims, also testified that truth had a distinct persona. In one such example, he spoke of himself, saying, *"I am ... the Truth."* (John 14.6) And in another place, he gave this teaching:

*"Howbeit when **he**, the Spirit of truth, is come, **he** will guide you into all truth: for **he** shall not speak of **himself**; but whatsoever **he** shall hear, that shall **he** speak: and **he** will show you things to come."* (John 16.13 bold emphasis and italics added)

In these statements, Jesus clearly gives *truth* the qualitative essence of a living, conscious personality—a persona with the ability to reason, educate, guide, and reveal truth. How does a Spirit bear witness, and how do we take a deposition from a Spirit? The answers to these questions were far beyond anything I could conjure up in my own mind. Yet, *God* was gracious to me. One of the questions I had to answer in my own mind was this – "If you believe that a spirit cannot give testimony; what do you base your belief on when you say the Scriptures are the words of *God*?" That was an impossible question to answer with logical reasoning.

Is it easy to distinguish between *Truth* and *Facts*? No; not at all; in fact, they can easily be compared to the features of identical twins. They may present an identical exterior, but will portray subtle and distinctive differences in character and personality to those who share their lives with them every day. It is much easier for someone who possesses a personal knowledge of the twins to point out those distinctions to the rest of us. So it is with Truth.

Here is an example of a fact, *"familiarity does not validate one's identity."* Most would be inclined to say this is a *true* statement. I have learned that a factual statement has enough credibility to be believable; yet, it is oftentimes later proven to be flawed or insufficient. Facts leave many unanswered questions, often leaving the answers to opinions and assumptions.

*Truth*, on the other hand, declares what is true and certain, not simply believable: it articulates those statements or doctrines that have been purged of all inaccuracy and error. *Truth* is the expert Witness who is impossible to contradict or refute; and whose testimony cannot be modified without degrading its flawlessness. *Truth*, by its nature is an eternally existent principle, consistent in its essential quality and character, and has the unique ability to create and regenerate life. The word of *God,* or *truth*, gives a seemingly insignificant life new meaning and purpose; excels human logic and understanding, brings into view the invisible words of deception, and exposes the intentions of one's heart.

*Truth* is the essence and convincing confirmation, the proof, that the distinguished persona of the Spirit of *God* is present. **His presence is manifested by his words—words** that typify a loving and gentle graciousness, a nurturing love, with an unadulterated perfection that can't be contradicted or overwhelmed. Some <u>believe</u> that <u>Truths</u> and <u>facts</u> are simply a matter of semantics, declaring they are synonymous and deny the existence of a major distinction. Here we go again with "beliefs".

*God*, in his infinite wisdom, gave Moses the insight to answer this question, *"<u>Can truth be fully ascertained?</u>"* Moses stated that *God* instructed him to <u>verify</u> every word of an allegation, accusation, and testimony to separate *Truth* from *Untruths*. He was given to understand that <u>Truth</u> is what is left of a testimony examined to the fullest extent, tried by fire, and whose remaining substance is free from defects.  Here is the statute that Moses presented:

> $^{12}$ If thou shalt hear say in one of thy cities, which the LORD thy *God* hath given thee to dwell there, saying,
> $^{13}$ Certain men, the children of Belial, are gone out from among you, and have withdrawn the inhabitants of their city, saying, Let us go and serve other *God*s, which ye have not known;
> **$^{14}$Then shalt thou inquire, and make search, and ask diligently;** *and, behold,* **if it be truth, and the thing certain,** that such abomination is wrought among you;
> $^{15}$Thou shalt surely smite the inhabitants of that city with the edge of the sword... (Deut. 13.12-15 emphasis added)

The New International Version of the Bible translates the fourteenth verse this way- *"Then you must* **inquire, probe** *and* **investigate it thoroughly.** *And if it is true and* **it has been proved** *that this detestable thing has been done among you ..."*

I will put this statement into modern language without changing its context—*"If someone tells you something, or accuses someone of an infraction, you must consider it to be hearsay until you can verify its inerrancy.  In order to validate their statements or allegations, a diligent inquiry shall be made of every witness, their testimonies subjected to an intense examination, scrutinized for any inaccuracy or lack of consistency, and impossible to disprove or contradict."*

Because malice, bias, jealousies, and outright falsehoods provoke charges and accusations that are less than truthful, the Lord instructed the elders to make a thorough examination of every witness' testimony. Soon after, the Israelites adopted the precept that every allegation had to be confirmed by the testimony of two or more witnesses.

Imagine this futuristic scenario—Arabs and Israelis are patiently and nervously awaiting a final verdict from the World Court in The Hague. This is a decision of critical importance—one that will have a permanent affect on their lives—a final decree that all have agreed will be permanently binding and recognized throughout the world. They await a ruling that will declare the name(s) of the rightful heir(s) to the land incorporated in Abraham's will, and the granting of legal title to the land. Does anyone believe for an instant the Palestinians and Israelis would not insist the court meticulously evaluate the integrity of all written and oral testimony with painstaking diligence, and persevere in their demand the Court examine them for any possible contradiction, ambiguity or flaw? Furthermore, if any were found, would they not be adamant about removing them from the record and from consideration; and persistent in their demands the Court's decision be based solely on the evidence that is incontrovertible?

I would not believe for a second either party would surrender the lot of their inheritance, if that was the decree, on anything less. If I were in a position to represent the Israeli or Palestinian people, I would never agree to surrender one inch of the land I truly believed belonged to my people based on "unfounded beliefs", and groundless details presented as evidence, or the ridiculous demand from an international envoy that I "accept by faith" the diplomat's judgment. And, I don't think they would agree to negotiate a peace accord subject to these arguments either.

An early Christian leader wrote these words; *"Now faith is the **substance** of things hoped for, the **evidence** of things not seen."* (Heb. 11.1 *emphasis added*) He reasoned that true faith contains substance; demonstrable evidence that something believed has factual merit and is based on valid proofs—not imagination, hearsay or theory. Somewhere in history, this lesson was replaced with—*Faith is simply a matter of believing, trusting with all your heart, without question or doubt*. This doctrine is far removed from the lessons taught by the prophets and apostles of old.

**Truth has a certain resonance, a discernible tone and recognizable expression and character** that Moses was given the ability to identify and distinguish. Truth exhibits a loving and gracious tender-heartedness, a kind, conciliatory manner, and never obscures an issue. Truth lacks bias and prejudice in judgment and is embellished with the meekness of charity which is quite distinctive in that it is unassuming, not easily provoked, not boisterous, arrogant, or prideful, never exalts itself, is not snobbish; and above all—reveals the inner beauty of the invisible *God* and *his* love.

**Truth can be compared to a strand of pure gold connecting one priceless pearl to another until it forms an elegantly styled necklace.** Pearls, however superior in quality, when separated, lack the majestic beauty they share collectively. Truth is confirmed in much the same way. Despite the uniqueness and inspiration "one single verse or statement" a Scripture may possess, we must take into consideration how it is used in the context of the lesson before we declare it to be the *truth*. The teaching cannot contradict a single verse in the rest of the Scriptures.

Like a strand of precious pearls, truth requires two or more harmonious statements, each one validating and supporting the other, until all the facts (pearls) are set in place. Once joined, they create an inseparable connection, a continuous bond that if broken by some outside source distorts its value, perfection, and beauty. The prophet Isaiah identified this principle: *"Whom shall he teach knowledge? And whom shall he make to understand doctrine? Them that are weaned from the milk, and drawn from the breasts. For precept must be upon precept, precept upon precept; line upon line, line upon line; here a little, and there a little:"* (Isa 28:9, 10 italics and quotation marks added)

This is an example of what I referred to earlier. After giving my testimony of how I came to identify truth, I referred back to the words of a prophet to confirm that what was revealed to me isn't something new; it is a truth taught some twenty five hundred years ago and is still valid today. If I examine the Covenant of Abraham with these precepts in mind, truth will be evident to all, and the proof of *truth* will be the joys that come with a sense of security and peace. One of the "proofs" science uses to determine if a living organism has life is its ability to move, which they refer to as *work*. Does truth *engage in work*? Of course it does. Truth separates, teaches, guides, and leads the servant of *God* in the ways of righteousness, reconciliation, and peace. Like chaff is separated from wheat, Truth also sets apart the servant of *God* from the servant of religion. How can we differentiate one from the other?

To begin with, if a man is a servant of *God*, he will have been called of *God* and instructed in the <u>*First Works of Truth*</u>, *reconciliation, restoration, and reunification of the lost with their Heavenly Father.* He will find himself engaged in a training regimen that will discipline him to remain focused on the challenge in front of him, the rescue, deliverance, and salvation of a lost soul. His skills will be honed until he has fully mastered the art of reconciliation. This is the primary work of *God* and it reveals the magnificence of *his* grace. The battle for the lost is fought with "swords of iron" against the sword of the Spirit, which is the Word of *God*. The "swords of iron" are verses from the holy books with which the enemies of *God*, the angels of death, use to confuse, overwhelm, and defeat the purpose of *God's* servant. This is why the Lord disciplines his servants to recognize the actual Voice and Word of *God*, and trains them to rightfully divide them from those verses being wielded by the enemy to keep the soul in bondage. In the end, the victorious servant of *God* presents the lost soul to the Father who finishes *his* mighty work of Salvation by reuniting the lost with *himself*. *In mercy, He* extends *his* arms to an enemy of the faith, a sinful unbeliever, and a soul long separated from *him*, one who is unworthy of the least of *his* tender mercies; yet, despite his rebellion, *God, our Holy Father in Heaven,* provides this lost soul an opportunity to be reconciled to *him,* rejoin *his* family, and receive *his* blessings. By the word of truth, his *Heavenly Father* gives the wayward son hope by removing judgment and condescension from *his* dialogue. Then, *he* initiates the process of transforming his meager hope into an enduring faith. The fulfillment of this "work" reveals the awesome beauty of *God's* grace. How can we not love *him* with all of our hearts after witnessing this kind of selfless love in action?

The servant of *God* is trained to use his *God*-given wisdom to resolve conflicts between contentious parties in order to free them from onerous resentments and enmity, and pave the way for the restoration of their relationship. He is like a celebrated gladiator in ancient days who found pleasure in his work, because his victories brought honour, joy, and glory to the *King.* The servant of *God* bears the gifts necessary to bring healing and support to those whose relationships have been damaged or broken. Once the soul is free of the turmoil that robbed its spirit of compassion, joy, love, and mercy, he is able to turn his attention to the worship of the Living *God* with a free spirit – the ultimate joy of victory!

Truth never stops working: is ever moving upon hearts, regenerating love and affection, reuniting loved ones, and restoring accord and balance. Can the "facts" accomplish the same goals? When we focus our attention on the "facts" associated with an offense, charity and grace are generally absent from the *negotiations.* We recall the others' faults and offenses from memory; relive the pain and anguish they "brought upon us"; repeat the offenses we accused them of, and make our demands for restitution or sincere apologies that are never fully accepted. Facts make the work of reconciliation much more difficult, if not altogether impossible. Recalling the events that has led to the Palestinians' current state of affairs; have they resulted in peace? No, and they never will.

Reconciliation is truly the primary work of every *God*-ordained ministry and is the rich by-product of *Truth's* successes—all other duties and services being secondary. Jesus of Nazareth alluded to this when he said, *"Therefore, if you are offering your gift at the altar and there remember that your brother has something against you; leave your gift there in front of the altar.* **First** *go and* **be reconciled** *to your brother; then come and offer your gift."* (Matt. 5.23-24 NIV) The Almighty gave his ministry permission to receive gifts offered to *God* – but according to Jesus, before our gift is accepted by *him*, we must, out of obedience to *his* will and submission to *his* word, first go and reconcile with our brother.

Plenty of evidence is given to support the premise that *Truth* has the characteristics of a vibrant personality, a living persona, who fosters unity, trust, love, peace and security. These works are in stark contrast to the works of deception and falsehood which promote division, jealousy, hatred, chaos, and hostility. It is taught that *God*'s word, identified as *Wisdom and Truth* by the prophets, created the heavens and the earth. Imagine the chaos and disorder all nature would endure if truth was a proponent of turmoil.

Contention and disagreement incite rebellion against the word of truth and its fruit provides energy for conflict and debate.

To recap, *Truth* <u>works</u> to reconcile conflicts and relationships, and is a true witness whose testimony can't be contradicted in any way. It only takes one valid sentence to contradict a witness' statements and invalidate volumes of testimony; but it takes many substantial statements to establish *Truth*. Regardless of which prophet or apostle's writings we decide to read, whether ancient or modern day, the source of their origin will be manifested by the *presence of the Golden strand of pure gold – the truth* that connects and forms a magnificent unbroken link between one irrefutable doctrine and another. It is this *Strand of Pure Gold* that reveals the heart and will of Almighty *God* and confirms the <u>*Truth*</u> that must be revealed to the Palestinians and Israelis before a resolution to the conflict in the Middle East can be amicably resolved.

I have given my testimony declaring my definitions and descriptions of truth. I have borne witness to how its power overwhelms the swords of the enemy, reconciles the lost to *God*, and reunites loved ones. I have declared that to discern the voice and tone of truth one must be disciplined to listen, focus on, and confirm that the person and "Voice" of *God* is present. This is my perception of truth, and its graces, as I have come to know and understand it. Truth has the same characteristics of the Almighty, whose work of love has circumcised my heart and soul to love *him* with all that is within me.

These precepts are the disciplines that I will employ to examine the Covenant, question every word and sentence if necessary, to ascertain its legitimacy, and to confirm that the "Voice", who revealed his truths to Moses, is the same "Voice" as the Testator, who contracted with Abraham. The *Voice*, if it is the *Word of God*, and *Truth*, will identify *himself* by revealing the "intentions of the hearts." And there will be no contradictions or inconsistencies.

This analysis will also affirm that this *Solution* is provided by the Lord to settle the conflicts between the brothers. Also, upon close examination, you will find my testimony to be void of personal beliefs and assumptions. Can the Covenant of Abraham sustain this type of scrutiny? I believe it can; but more importantly, I believe it must, in order to avoid an ominous cataclysm in the Middle East.

The *Voice of God*, the alleged *autho*r of the Covenant will give us all the keys we need to unlock the truths that have been withheld for generations. Will the *Voice* confirm that the Palestinians are entitled to share the inheritance with Israel? We will be able to witness how his proofs are exposed. Until these *truths* are revealed, neither of the families will ever accept a negotiated settlement for Palestine; not to mention Jerusalem; and I can't fault them. In addition, the triggers will remain in place and the hostilities will continue unabated.

## *QUESTIONABLE ISSUES*

I must draw attention to some issues that may easily fall under the heading, *Acceptance by Faith,* and result in some contradictions:

• First, I am only introducing and examining that portion of the Hebrew Scriptures that reveal more details of the Covenant made between *God* and Abraham, than any other writings to which I am privy.

• Secondly, there are no living witnesses to provide evidence that Abraham and Moses actually had any conversations with the *Deity* they identified as *God Almighty* or *the God of Abraham* during their lifetime. This is a matter of faith that cannot be verified.

• Thirdly, the Covenant was written more than six centuries after the death of Abraham; obviously, there were no living witnesses that could bear witness to the accuracy of the detailed description contained in the Mosaic account. This is also a matter of faith and unverifiable.

These are not issues up for debate by either party. It is my understanding both families are satisfied the persons and statements described in the Covenant are irrefutable; and as proof of their convictions, they have included them in their Sacred Scriptures and in their teachings, which they deem to be holy and true. Hence, to argue these positions would only cast a shadow on the respective religions, which is not my intent or desire. However, there are certain doctrinal beliefs they do not share common ground on. These are matters of *faith* that have served to disunite them—and are subjects which I will not engage in, nor take sides with, for reasons I will note.

- **The Proper Name of *God*** – I am using the English versions of the Mosaic texts. Hence, I am deliberately avoiding any preferential Hebrew or Islamic names for *God*. In the English versions, there are no discernible statements contained in the writing of the Covenant indicating the name, or identity of *God,* as used by these religious bodies today. Therefore, for the single purpose of this writing, when I use the words, *Lord, Lord God*, or *God*, the deity I will be referring to is none other than the *God of Abraham*, or *God Almighty*. These were the names of *God* Moses identified with as he related the details of the Covenant.

- **The True Religion** - the Covenant does not mention or identify an established religion or preferred practice of a religion ordained by *God*. Therefore, I will not be identifying Abraham with any particular religious sect or denomination that he *may have been a part of* in order to maintain the integrity of all available facts.

It is also my understanding that both Judaism and Islam include some form of these affirmations of *God* in their doctrinal professions of faith*:* *He is All Knowing, All Truth, Pure and Holy, Perfect in Knowledge and Wisdom, incapable of lying, being deceived, or making an error in speech or judgment.*

These affirmations of "Faith" are critical to the eventual outcome of this work because they identify the nature and character of *God* as declared by the sons of Abraham; and because of their importance, I will be making use of them repeatedly, to substantiate or sanction "the Truth" of all statements made on behalf of **"The Covenant."**

Another contentious issue may involve my decision to evaluate the Covenant as a *legal* document apart from its "religious significance". I maintain the position that when the Covenant was created, it was intended to be a "legally" binding contract, an arrangement which I intend to prove beyond any doubt. Whenever two or more individuals decide to make an Agreement, such as a Will or Deed, particularly one that includes the conveyance of real estate or other valuable assets, reduce the contract to writing, and then publicize it: they have put the "world" on notice the transaction took place between the parties named within, and they have mutually agreed to its terms and substance. By creating a public record of the transaction, they make known that it is their intent to assure it has *legal standing* in the event anyone challenged its legitimacy, or might lay claim to the land that was part of the transaction. Since there is an ongoing dispute as to whether the Palestinians lack "standing" as to their claim of entitlement to the land previously known as Canaan, the only resolution to the problem must be found in the public document allegedly made between *God* and Abraham. This is the issue at the heart of conflict.

Now, we know there are valid and invalid contracts, wills, and deeds. The question is what is needed to establish legitimacy? Is it considered authentic because it bears the seal of a certain prophet, religious or political leader? No; a valid document must contain certain criteria that include enough information to ascertain its intent.

For example, a Will must contain **the identity of all parties beginning with the Testator and include the exact name(s) of his heir(s).** Usually, a Will that includes real estate will contain a concise description of the metes and bounds, or specific landmarks to the parcel. The text may also include other provisions, restrictions, critical dates, **Contingencies, or an Opt-out Clause** requiring the heir(s) to perform an obligation or duty before he can receive his portion of the inheritance. It may also contain penalties that would limit the inheritor's rights if he fails to fulfill some required action. The document may grant a provision to remedy a **Default** as well. Finally, whenever possible, the document should be witnessed by, and/or **sealed,** by a third party. Ancient documents, or Wills, did not necessarily contain all of these elements, but they had to contain the most important ones, specifically, the names of the parties, the exact name(s) of the heir(s), the explicit name of the owner(s) of the property being transferred, and an accurate description of the personal or real property conveyed. Are we able to find these details in the Covenant of Abraham?

- **Identification of the parties**:

   The *Testator* - "***God* Almighty**;"
   The *Inheritor*- **"Abraham,"**

- **Tangible Property: "The whole land of Canaan"**

- **Length of Contract:** "an everlasting covenant."

- **Contingency** – "... <u>*and I will be their God.*</u>" *(May also be properly translated as-)* "... *and I <u>must be</u> their God.*"

The Covenant contains the most important elements present in a legally binding Will or contract. Of greater importance, keep in mind Moses testified that *God* revealed the Covenant to him on Mt. Sinai. He reduced the Covenant to writing to publicize its existence to the seed of Abraham. Furthermore, Moses made it very clear to the Israelites there were conditions they had to meet before *God* would fulfill *his* part in the Covenant. Therefore, my contention is this; assuming his testimony is true in that *God* was the *One* who created the Covenant, revealed the Covenant, and ordered Moses to publicize it; the Covenant should withstand every possible challenge to its validity; and the presence of its *truth* should verify whether *God* is the *Creator* and *Author* of the Covenant with Abraham.

**Let me say this for the record: if I can't find and validate the essence of *God* in the Covenant, you would not be reading this book right now, because it would have never been written.**

There are many who would take offense at this work because it promises to reveal the hidden agenda that has succeeded in keeping the hostilities between Isaac and Ishmael alive. But *God* has given me a charge to write this book for the sole benefit of the Palestinians and those Israelis who seek truth, to bring light, hope, and the possibility of a peaceful future for their children.

To my knowledge, the Covenant is the only document either party can present to sustain a claim they are the rightful heirs to Abraham's estate, and the land of Canaan. Naturally, I do not intend to argue every point an unbeliever may raise to question the validity of the Bible, Torah, or Qur'an. Atheists, denominationalists, humanists, and others will only believe what they *choose to believe*, and will argue incessantly against Truth. Their history over the last five thousand years has substantiated this fact.

## *MOSES' ENCOUNTER WITH GOD*

Moses testified that his first encounter with *God* took place on Mt. Sinai where he claimed to have heard *the voice of God.* This presents two reasonable questions: first, if Moses never had a prior experience with *God*, how could he insist the voice was actually that of *God?* Secondly, presuming he never saw the face of *God* how could he confirm *his* identity? These questions require plausible answers at least.

In Moses' defence, many have argued that belief in *God* is a matter of faith and can't be proven; declaring that no one can confirm the reality of *God* and any attempt to do so is an exercise in futility. If what they say is true, then it is impossible to conclude—who was (were) the heir(s) given the Right to Inherit Abraham's estate, and there would be no rationale for me to go forward with this book.

For Moses, or his following, to simply state they *believed* the "Voice" was that of *God* doesn't make their claim reliable or defensible. If Moses had nothing more than his *beliefs* to establish the identity of the *Voice*, it would be impossible for him, or anyone else, to validate the claim that *God* was the *One* who actually spoke to him and revealed that it was *he* who entered into a Covenant with Abraham centuries earlier. Secondly, if Moses only heard the "Voice" once, no one would believe he could identify the *"*Voice of *God"* in the first place. So, am I saying that I reject his testimony? No, I am simply pointing out some preliminary questions that require reasonable answers before I can examine the Covenant.

Since the testimony, whether penned by Moses or dictated to a scribe, was written some six hundred years after the death of Abraham, I need to verify its origin if at all possible. Did he receive it from *God*, or a third party? I must make every attempt to ascertain the identity of the "Voice". In Moses' account of the events that took place in Egypt and at the crossing of the Red Sea, he had occasion to hear this "Voice" many times and, with the proofs he witnessed with his own eyes, he concluded that it was none other than *God* who spoke to him. It is logical to deduce that the person Moses identified as *God* and the "*LORD*" was discernible to him by certain distinctive and familiar expressions, characteristics, and consistencies in language and tone.

Unlike an assumption, I base a conclusive statement on reliable information. Science has concluded that every living thing has a unique sound, pitch, tone, expression, and rhythm distinctive to its own genre and individuality. If we acknowledge *God* to be a living being, as most believers do, *he* also must have distinguishing characteristics. Let us read Moses' eye witness account of his encounter with *God* as it is recorded in the Biblical book of Exodus:

> [1]Now Moses kept the flock of Jethro his father in law, the priest of Midian: and he led the flock to the backside of the desert, and came to the mountain of *God*, even to Horeb.
> [2]And **the angel of the LORD** appeared unto him in a flame of fire out of the midst of a bush: and he looked, and, behold, the bush burned with fire, and the bush was not consumed.

> ³And Moses said, I will now turn aside, and see this great sight, why the bush is not burnt.
> ⁴And when **the LORD** saw that he turned aside to see, **_God_** called unto him out of the midst of the bush, and said, Moses, Moses. And he said, Here am I.
> ⁵And he said, Draw not nigh hither: put off thy shoes from off thy feet, for the place whereon thou standest is holy ground.
> ⁶Moreover he said, **I am the _God_ of thy father, the _God_ of Abraham, the _God_ of Isaac, and the _God_ of Jacob.** And Moses hid his face; for he was afraid to look upon *God*.      (Ex. 3.1-6 emphasis added)

As we see, within the same paragraph the *persona* is identified as an *angel*, the *LORD,* and as *God*. To debate whether it was *God, himself,* who appeared to Moses, is ludicrous because it is safe to say no one alive today could distinguish one from the other. Moses was prevented from seeing the face of *God, but even if he had seen his face,* he couldn't testify with any certainty the person he saw was *God*, or an angel. How would he know the difference? He testified that the *angel* identified *himself* as *God*. Could he say with absolute certainty that the voice he often heard was actually *God's Voice,* and deny any possibility the "Voice" could have been that of the angel? No; of course not. Moses could only testify to the following: that the "Voice" he heard on the mountaintop identified *himself* as *God;* and the *Voice* had the same recognizable tone and familiarities every time he heard it; and furthermore, as he obeyed the commands the "Voice" gave him, the *power* of *its* word was undeniable when the judgments against the Egyptians were executed before his eyes. So, whether we choose to believe it was *God* or an *angel* is not important. The most important consideration is whether the words and expressions uttered by the "Voice" were consistent, absent of contradiction, and identifiable to Moses.

If people call us by a name different from our birth name, is our identity altered or compromised in any way? Does it change our character, nature, manner of speaking, and habitual behavior? No, they remain the same. Abu Mazen and Mahmoud Abbas is the same person, retaining the same personal traits; therefore, it is more important that we can recognize the man than to argue over his name.

There are some remaining questions which must be answered individually. Does Moses acknowledge that the *God* he came to know and identify with was *Merciful and Loving, Tender-hearted, Perfect in Wisdom, Understanding* and *Judgment, Gracious, and Incapable of Error and Foolish Talk,* etc.? If so, we should have no difficulty identifying the Testator in the Covenant of Promise by way of *his* "Voice", or words. As I have said before, neither Islam nor Judaism are arguing the identity or reality of *God* as *he* revealed *himself* to Moses.

It is certainly possible this issue was brought before certain wise judges among their ancestors who were unable to confirm the identity of *God* from a *legal* standpoint. If this did occur, I am certain they would have deferred the debate to the religious leaders rather than delegitimize the Covenant. Perhaps that is how this issue became a religious argument in the first place. I don't have any proof this statement is valid, but it does raise an interesting question.

Let me make this point clear once again; I am focusing my attention on the *Testator* in the Covenant, not arguing religious faith. If the words Moses attributes to *God* are inconsistent, confusing, or conflicting, a significant question presents itself that may potentially nullify the possibility the Covenant could be resolved in a legal setting. This would have devastating consequences; in that the issue would remain irresolvable and leave the question of inheritance rights to the religions who will *accept their own doctrines by faith,* and continue to foster the hostilities from generation to generation without hope of a peaceful end. For this reason, I must maintain a conscientious and deliberate focus on the direct quotes Moses attributes to <u>God</u>. In so doing, I will be able to arrive at one of two conclusions— the existence and nature of Almighty *God is present;* or, there are irregularities or contradictions that are inconsistent with the characteristics of *God*.

There is another question of significance I must bring to the forefront. If the voice was that of *God*, whom we've said is incapable of error in speech or judgment, why did *he* not also include the name of Abraham's firstborn, Ishmael, when *he* identified *himself* to Moses? Moses quoted *him* as saying, "... **I am the God of thy father, the God of Abraham, the God of Isaac, and the God of Jacob."** (Ex. 3.6 emphasis added) (Interesting observation that raises more questions indeed).

According to Moses' account, he discovered that he was a descendant of Levi, the son of Jacob, the grandson of Isaac, and of course, the great grandson of Abraham, before he left Egypt. Did *God* identify *himself* to Moses as *he* did because it was important to Moses to know his true paternal lineage, as some have asserted? Since nothing is written to substantiate this position, I have to consider it conjecture. However, we do know Abraham had two sons of prominent mention, Ishmael, the elder, and Isaac, the younger. In addition, he had several more sons by Keturah, his wife of some thirty years, after Sarah's death. One of Keturah's sons, Midian, was the father of Jethro, the priest of Midian, with whom Moses resided after his exile from Egypt. Is it possible Jethro revealed his kinship to Moses and declared he was also a son of Abraham? It would seem likely, but again we don't have any testimony upon which to rely.

Moses spent forty years in Midian, married the daughter of Jethro and fathered two sons, all of whom were under Jethro's tutorage. Perhaps, it was Jethro through whom Moses received his "education and introduction" to the family of Abraham and his *God*. But, that doesn't give us the rationale for Ishmael being left out of *God's* initial introduction at this point. Some have made the claim that Abraham's sons, born of Hagar and Keturah, turned away from the *God of Abraham* and were excommunicated. This is a radical twist from the written account of Moses. Upon his return from Egypt, he gave an account to Jethro, of all the magnificent events that *God* had performed to liberate the children of Israel from under the bondage of Pharaoh:

¹When Jethro, the priest of Midian, Moses' father in law, heard of all that **_God_** had done for Moses, and for Israel his people, and that **the LORD** had brought Israel out of Egypt;

²Then Jethro, Moses' father in law, took Zipporah, Moses' wife, after he had sent her back,

³And her two sons; of which the name of the one was Gershom; for he said, I have been an alien in a strange land:

⁴And the name of the other was Eliezer; for the _God_ of my father, said he, was mine help, and delivered me from the sword of Pharaoh:

⁵And Jethro, Moses' father in law, came with his sons and his wife unto Moses into the wilderness, where he encamped at the mount of _God_:

⁶And he said unto Moses, I thy father in law Jethro am come unto thee, and thy wife, and her two sons with her.

⁷And Moses went out to meet his father in law, and did obeisance, and kissed him; and they asked each other of their welfare; and they came into the tent.

⁸And Moses told his father in law all that **the LORD** had done unto Pharaoh and to the Egyptians for Israel's sake, and all the travail that had come upon them by the way, and how the LORD delivered them.

⁹**And Jethro rejoiced for all the goodness which the LORD had done to Israel,** whom he had delivered out of the hand of the Egyptians.

> ¹⁰And Jethro said, blessed be the LORD, who hath delivered you out of the hand of the Egyptians, and out of the hand of Pharaoh, who hath delivered the people from under the hand of the Egyptians.
> ¹¹Now I know that **the LORD** is greater than all *Gods*: for in the thing wherein they dealt proudly he was above them.
> ¹²And Jethro, Moses' father in law, took a burnt offering and sacrifices for *God*: and Aaron came, and all the elders of Israel, to eat bread with Moses' father in law before *God.*
> (Ex. 18:1-12 emphasis added)

*And, "Jethro rejoiced for all the goodness which **the LORD** had done to Israel...."* (vs. 9) This was the brother whom they had not seen in more than four hundred years! Secondly, he gave due honor and worship to ***God,*** offering up sacrifices and offerings to *him*, (typically, sacrifices for sin, thanksgiving, and peace offerings). In this account, all the elders of Israel had no objection to worshipping with Jethro and eating with him before *God*. It would appear, though not written, the Israelites did not detect any noteworthy difference between their own customs of worship and those of the Midianites; neither did they have reason to believe they were worshipping any other than the *God* of their father, Abraham. Keep in mind now, this event took place more than four hundred years after the Ishmaelites had any contact with their brothers, the Israelites.

In time, for reasons that may be ascertainable, the Ishmaelites were somehow labeled by the Jews, and later by the Christians, as cast-offs of the *God* of Abraham based on a charge of idolatry. Perhaps there is testimony that will bear witness to this, but thus far, the evidence Moses gives us doesn't support these claims. I can't argue against any data which supports the claim the Midianites and other descendants of Abraham <u>did</u> turn to other gods, Israel being one of them. However, the only time period I am dealing with, and examining in this book, is Abraham's era—the time during which the Covenant was made—and the short time period after Moses was made aware of its existence. The written history that we have for this time period does not support or substantiate these claims.

If there was a premeditated decision to disinherit Ishmael: the question is - who made it, *God*, Abraham, or another? Surely, the children of Israel would view *God's failure* to recognize Ishmael as a distinct act of contempt, abandonment, and/or excommunication; and as such, he would be ineligible to receive or claim any portion of his father's estate. *God's* silence on the subject would have encouraged Israelis to adopt a false belief. This certainly isn't consistent with the character of a *God* who has the reputation of being pure, holy, and perfect in wisdom in all *his* ways. Can we find an actual quotation within this time period to confirm the idea that Ishmael was disinherited? If so, and the quote was attributed to *God,* then there isn't anything amiss in *God's* salutation to Moses. If not, something is definitely wrong. Let's take a closer look at the statements *God* made to Moses relating to the Covenant.

## *GOD'S BLESSING TO ABRAHAM*

> "Now the LORD had said unto Abram, Get thee out of thy country, and from thy kindred, and from thy father's house, unto a land that I will show thee: And I will make of thee a great nation, and I will bless thee, and make thy name great; and thou shalt be a blessing: And I will bless them that bless thee, and curse him that curseth thee: and in thee shall all families of the earth be blessed."
> (Gen. 12.1-3 emphasis added)

*God* revealed to Moses that *he* spoke to Abraham, chose him over all other potential "righteous men" on earth, commanded him to leave his father's house and country, and journey to another land. Once he arrived in this new country, *God* would begin to execute *his* promises. Why did *God* require Abraham to leave his family and homeland in the first place? Joshua, the successor to Moses, gathered the people together and said, "This is what the LORD, the *God* of Israel, says: *'Long ago your forefathers, including Terah the father of Abraham and Nahor, lived beyond the River and worshipped other gods. But I took your father Abraham from the land beyond the River and led him throughout Canaan and gave him many descendants."* (Josh. 24. 2, 3 NIV emphasis added).

This statement is consistent with other Scriptures in both the Torah and Quran in which we find evidence of the Lord's refusal to bless people and lands who worship any other but the True *God*. Apparently, *God* considered the land, and all that was in it, unclean. Therefore, in order for

Abraham to receive *God's* blessing, he had to remove himself from the land of his upbringing, abandon any property, inheritance, or other entitlements, and leave his family behind because they worshipped false gods. Abraham may have been a nonconformist with the courage to refuse the demands he worship a *god* that could not substantiate its existence. We do not have any history to substantiate this; but we have to wonder how he came to know and identify with the True *God* when his father raised him to worship false *gods*. The Scriptures do not tell us; however, it is interesting to note that God also caused Moses to surrender his authority, property, and any future inheritance he may have been entitled to in Egypt, as well. *He* then initiated a series of events to remove him from a people that worshipped false gods; and after delivering the children of Israel from under Pharaoh's hand, led them to the land of promise. So far, the methods and reasoning used by the *Voice* are consistent.

***"And I will make of thee a great nation, and I will bless thee, and make thy name great;"*** (Gen. 12.2 - emphasis added) Even more extraordinary is the next promise, because there is no record that *God* made this promise to anyone other than Abraham. *"... and **you shall be a blessing**; and I will bless them that bless thee, and curse him that curseth thee: **and in thee shall all families of the earth be blessed.**"* (Gen. 12.3 – emphasis added)

Every blessing promised and imputed by *God* is predicated upon the performance of some action or on the integrity of one's heart. Here are two examples: *"If you fully obey the LORD your God and carefully follow all his commands I give you today... all these blessings will come upon you and accompany you if you obey the LORD your God":* (Deut. 28.1,2 NIV emphasis added) <u>This verse requires acts of obedience and observance</u> before a blessing is given. In another verse, it is written, *"Blessed are the meek: for they shall inherit the earth."* (Matt. 5.5) <u>Meekness is a quality or virtue</u> abiding within one's heart.

I am raising this question: if **Abraham *is the blessing*, or is to be the blessing**—how do we receive it? How can we receive Abraham? How is Abraham and the blessing upon him imputed to us—by an act of obedience—the integrity of our heart—or both? The facts would indicate that *God* recognized Abraham's obedience and mentioned it in *his* decision to bless him. However, truth says, "God did not demand his obedience to law as a requirement to *receive* the blessing." In the words of *God*, (Gen. 18.19), *he* knew Abraham would command his descendants to comply with the principles of justice and equity that he practiced. God could command, (and he did according to Moses), the people be just and equitable; however, the principles of justice and equity are virtues that are practiced in one's daily life, not just in obedience to a written statement or doctrine. The implication here is that a virtuous heart is needful. In addition, a decision to bless Abraham or his children would have to be motivated by a heart tempered by the Spirit of *God*.

If this statement is factual, we should expect the children of Abraham to exhibit an inner virtue, integrity, and benevolence, which would be ascertainable apart from their willful obedience to religious law and dogma. Abraham's blessing will be "imputed" to those who bless him (and /or his children). In Hebrew, the root word for *impute* means *to weave* or *to plait* (braid). The use of this word gives rise to the concept that *God's* blessing upon Abraham is a type of covering, likened to an elaborate shawl or tightly braided headpiece.

We can find another example of this in the tale of Elijah who passed his mantle to Elisha. By this action, Elijah transferred his authority, consecration, and the blessings imputed to him by *God* to Elisha to continue his work and assume responsibility for teaching his disciples. The transfer of blessing is sanctioned in the next part - ***"All families on earth will be blessed in you."*** (Gen. 12.3 emphasis added)—not in the actual person or embodiment of Abraham himself, but under the shroud or mantle *God* bestowed upon him.

This "shawl of blessing" is available to **all families on earth;** a phrase that includes all nations and people that believe in the *God* of Abraham, and whose hearts share the faith and virtues *God* found pleasing in Abraham, faith, integrity, steadfast fidelity, and dedication to obedience and devotion to *God. God* named these people the "seed of Abraham." How do we reckon those whose genealogy descends from Abraham but practice evil and injustice? Should we count them among the children of Abraham?

In the Quran, we find this verse: *"And when his Lord tried Ibrahim with certain words, he fulfilled them. He said: "Surely I will make you an Imam of men. Ibrahim said: And of my offspring?* ***My covenant does not include the unjust****, said He."* (Surah 2.124 – emphasis added)

The predecessor to Jesus of Nazareth, a prophet known as John the Baptist, had this to say to support this perception: John said to the crowds coming out to be baptized by him; *"O generation of vipers, who hath warned you to flee from the wrath to come? Bring forth therefore fruits worthy of repentance, and begin not to say within yourselves, we have Abraham to our father: for I say unto you, that God is able of these stones to raise up children unto Abraham. And now also the ax is laid unto the root of the trees: every tree therefore which bringeth not forth good fruit is hewn down, and cast into the fire."* (Luke 3.7-9 emphasis added).

The Lord, as recorded in the Quran, and Jesus' disciple, John, made it clear that being a natural descendent of Abraham did not grant anyone special privileges or entitlements. With these words, they indicated that it was the intent and fulfillment of the motivations within one's heart that allowed them to claim their descendancy, not their genealogy. John emphasized the meaning of his words when he said, (I am paraphrasing*) "If God wanted children with hardened hearts to be counted as the seed of Abraham, He could create them out of these stones."*

From these statements, we can conclude that the **"descendants of Abraham" are those whose hearts yield to the principles *God* ordained and are moved to fulfill these precepts by virtue of the integrity with which *God* filled their hearts.**

These assertions are consistent with Moses' account of what *God* required of all *His* children*: "And thou shalt love the LORD thy God with all thine heart, and with all thy soul, and with all thy might. And these words, which I* *command thee this day, shall be in thine heart: And thou shalt teach them diligently unto thy children, and shalt talk of them when thou sittest in thine house, and when thou walkest by the way, and when thou liest down, and when thou risest up."* (Deut. 6.5-7 emphasis added)

In the following verses (which will be necessary to recall a little later) Moses reveals the virtues and the effects that Abraham's integrity will have on his children: *"And the LORD said, Shall I hide from Abraham that thing which I do; seeing that Abraham shall surely become a great and mighty nation, and all the nations of the earth shall be blessed in him? For I know him, that he will command his children and his household after him, and they shall keep the way of the LORD, to do justice and judgment; that the LORD may bring upon Abraham that which he hath spoken of him."* (Gen. 18.17-19 emphasis added)

I have taken the liberty to offer the following paraphrase to this verse in order to provide a clearer and richer meaning consistent with other statements attributed to *God*.

"The children of Abraham shall maintain customs, establish laws, and moral ethics of daily life consistent with the accepted practices *God* would have them live by. They will establish a system of justice; and a judicial process that requires every law and statute be executed with equity and impartiality for all. They will not regard one's financial worth, or social and political status; for they consider the practice of receiving bribes or gifts to sway judicial decisions abhorrent, and value the blessings and mercies of *God* above all material possessions."

So far, we have seen no inconsistency in the words attributed to *God*. *"And the LORD said unto Abram, after that Lot was separated from him, "Lift up now thine eyes, and look from the place where thou art northward, and southward, and eastward, and westward:* **For all the land which thou seest, to thee will I give it, and to thy seed for ever. And I will make thy seed as the dust of the earth:** *so that if a man can number the dust of the earth, then shall thy seed also be numbered."* (Gen. 13.14-16 quotations and emphasis added)

> [1]After these things the word of the LORD came unto Abram in a vision, saying, Fear not, Abram: I am thy shield, and thy exceeding great reward.
> [2]And Abram said, Lord *God*, what wilt thou give me, seeing I go childless, and the steward of my house is this Eliezer of Damascus?
> [3]And Abram said, Behold, to me thou hast given no seed: and, lo, one born in my house is mine heir.
> [4]And, behold, the word of the LORD came unto him, saying, **This shall not be thine heir; but he that shall come forth out of thine own bowels shall be thine heir.**
> [5]And he brought him forth abroad, and said, Look now toward heaven, and tell the stars, if thou be able to number them: and he said unto him, So shall thy seed be.
> [6]And he believed in the LORD; and he counted it to him for righteousness.

> ⁷And he said unto him, I am the LORD that brought thee out of Ur of the Chaldees, to give thee this land to inherit it. (Gen. 15.1-7)
>
> ¹³And he said unto Abram, **Know of a surety that thy seed shall be a stranger in a land that is not theirs, and shall serve them; and they shall afflict them four hundred years;**
> ¹⁴And also that nation, whom they shall serve, will I judge: and afterward shall they come out with great substance. (Gen. 15.13, 14)
>
> ¹⁸In the same day the LORD made a covenant with Abram, saying, **Unto thy seed have I given this land, from the river of Egypt unto the great river, the river Euphrates:**
> ¹⁹The Kenites, and the Kenizzites, and the Kadmonites,
> ²⁰ And the Hittites, and the Perizzites, and the Rephaims,
> ²¹And the Amorites, and the Canaanites, and the Girgashites, and the Jebusites.
> (Gen. 15.18-21 emphasis added)

Here is where the debates begin which cast a shadow upon the identity of *God,* as Moses declared *him.* Up to this point, the only significant "fact" we can draw upon, that was included in Moses' account, is that *God* spoke of Abraham's seed without naming any of his, ***yet unborn, children.*** Still, many argue the succeeding verses clearly indicate the "seed" of whom *God* spoke.

The Jews believe *God* made this promise as a future reference to Isaac alone; however, we cannot validate their position from this passage. In fact, the argument conflicts with the quotation because the descendants of Isaac have never, in their entire history, reached a population as great as stated in the passage. Besides, years later, Moses made this statement to the children of Israel. *"The LORD did not set his love upon you, nor choose you, because ye were more in number than any people; for ye were the fewest of all people:"* (Deut. 7.7 italics added). This verse supports the position that *God* did not fulfill this promise in Isaac if we use the population as a proof.

There are four major doctrinal positions regarding the identity of the seed of Abraham. The first, Isaac is the heir of promise; the second, Ishmael is the legitimate heir of promise; third, Abraham had more than one son, and therefore, *God's* statement included both sons and their future generations collectively; lastly, *God* included Abraham's concubines and the children of his slaves in addition to his two sons. Do we have conclusive evidence to justify one of these arguments to the exclusion of the others? Actually, none of them is completely true as stated.

*"This shall not be thine **heir**; but **he** that shall come forth out of thine own bowels shall be thine **heir**."* One who accepts things *by faith* may ask, "What other way can this verse be interpreted? The entire text clearly indicates that *God* is speaking of one "single" individual, a single heir. *'Know of a surety that thy **seed** shall be a **stranger** in a land that is not theirs....'* The word, **'stranger,'** in the singular adds to the position that *God* was telling Abraham

that from his loins **one son** would be born who would be the heir apparent to the covenants of promise—which included the land of Canaan in its entirety!" This sounds factual, or at least plausible, but is it the Truth?

What we do know is this—Abraham had at least two sons, neither of which *God* specifically named <u>at this point</u>. Ishmael's descendants argue that his progeny has achieved the massive numbers spoken of by *God*, and that they have lived on the lands between the Nile and the Euphrates for thousands of years. However, they still have not reconciled the fact that *God* spoke of the seed of Abraham being enslaved for four hundred years. If Ishmael could prove that Pharaoh enslaved <u>him</u>, his case would be virtually indisputable. However, the Quran also refers to Israel's bondage in Egypt, not Ishmael's. Despite the strong arguments made by the sons, their testimony (at the moment) is both unconvincing and refutable. I repeat: I cannot make a determination of truth by what someone *chooses* to believe. Truth is self-supportive; and reveals itself after an intense examination that leaves nothing to chance, assumption, or rebuttal.

From what is written, I can only glean the following facts: 1) *God* spoke of Abraham's seed and his progeny before they were born; 2) *he* predicted a period of four centuries Abraham's descendants would be servants in another land; 3) *he* promised the land to Abraham and his ***seed (children)*** as an inheritance before he fathered his first child; 4) the seed of Abraham would become too numerous to count and would occupy the lands between the Nile and the Euphrates.

Soon after the Lord made this promise to Abraham, Sarah was "moved" to lend her slave-girl, Hagar, to her husband so he may have an heir from his own loins. There is no doubt in my mind that Abraham thought this was the only way *God's* plan would be fulfilled because Sarah was barren. The following year, Hagar gave birth to his first son, whom he named Ishmael. *"And Sarai said unto Abram, Behold now, the LORD hath restrained me from bearing: I pray thee, go in unto my maid; it may be that I may obtain children by her. And Abram hearkened to the voice of Sarai. And he went in unto Hagar, and she conceived:"* (Gen. 16.2, 4)

With this information in mind, the communication between *God* and Abraham will be a little clearer. I present here a copy of the Covenant in its entirety.

## THE COVENANT

¹And when Abram was ninety years old and nine, the LORD appeared to Abram, and said unto him, **I am the Almighty *God*;** walk before me, and be thou perfect.

²And I will make my covenant between me and thee, and will multiply thee exceedingly.

³And Abram fell on his face: and *God* talked with him, saying,

⁴**As for me**, behold, **my covenant is with thee, and thou shalt be a father of many nations.**

⁵Neither shall thy name any more be called Abram, but **thy name shall be Abraham**; for a father of many nations have I made thee.

⁶And I will make thee exceeding fruitful, and I will make nations of thee, and kings shall come out of thee.

⁷**And I will establish my covenant between me and thee and thy seed after thee in their generations for an everlasting covenant,** to be a *God* unto thee, and to thy seed after thee.

⁸**And I will give unto thee, and to thy seed after thee, the land wherein thou art a stranger, all the land of Canaan, for an everlasting possession; and** I will be their *God.*

⁹And *God* said unto Abraham, Thou shalt keep my covenant therefore, thou, and thy seed after thee in their generations.

¹⁰This is my covenant, which ye shall keep, between me and you and thy seed after thee; Every man child among you shall be circumcised.

¹¹And ye shall circumcise the flesh of your foreskin; and it shall be a token of the covenant betwixt me and you.

¹²And he that is eight days old shall be circumcised among you, every man child in your generations, he that is born in the house, or bought with money of any stranger, which is not of thy seed.

¹³He that is born in thy house, and he that is bought with thy money, must needs be circumcised: and my covenant shall be in your flesh for an everlasting covenant.

¹⁴And the uncircumcised man child whose flesh of his foreskin is not circumcised, that soul shall be cut off from his people; he hath broken my covenant.

¹⁵And *God* said unto Abraham, As for Sarai thy wife, thou shalt not call her name Sarai, but **Sarah shall her name be.**

¹⁶And I will bless her, and give thee a son also of her: yea, I will bless her, and she shall be a mother of nations; kings of people shall be of her.

¹⁷Then Abraham fell upon his face, and laughed, and said in his heart, Shall a child be born unto him that is an hundred years old? and shall Sarah, that is ninety years old, bear?

¹⁸And Abraham said unto *God*, O that Ishmael might live before thee!

¹⁹And *God* said, **Sarah thy wife shall bear thee a son indeed; and thou shalt call his name Isaac:**

and I will establish my covenant with him for an everlasting covenant and with his seed after him.
**²⁰And as for Ishmael, I have heard thee: Behold, I have blessed him, and will make him fruitful, and will multiply him exceedingly; twelve princes shall he beget, and I will make him a great nation.**
*²¹But my covenant will I establish with Isaac,* which **Sarah shall bear unto thee** **at this set time in the next year.**
²²And he left off talking with him, and *God* went up from Abraham.
²³And Abraham took Ishmael his son, and all that were born in his house, and all that were bought with his money, every male among the men of Abraham's house; and circumcised the flesh of their foreskin in the selfsame day, as *God* had said unto him.
²⁴And Abraham was ninety years old and nine, when he was circumcised in the flesh of his foreskin.
²⁵And Ishmael his son was thirteen years old, when he was circumcised in the flesh of his foreskin.
²⁶In the selfsame day was Abraham circumcised, and Ishmael his son.
²⁷And all the men of his house, born in the house, and bought with money of the stranger, were circumcised with him. (Gen. 17.1-27 emphasis added)

Let us examine the main elements of the Covenant, the execution of which is contingent upon Abraham and his seed agreeing to fulfill certain conditions. In fact, it is better to say they **must make three separate and deliberate decisions** before God will fulfill the promises *he* outlines in the Covenant.

When Abram was ninety-nine years old, the LORD appeared to him and said, ***"I am God Almighty; walk before me and be blameless**, and, I will make my covenant between me and you, and will multiply you exceedingly."*** Take notice: *God* first identifies *himself* by name; (*he* also identified *himself* when *he* met Moses on the mount) and in the fifth verse declares the name Abram will be forever identified: *"Neither shall thy name any more be called Abram, but thy name shall be Abraham."* Identification of the parties to a *Will and Testament is* of vital importance. Then *he states the first of three conditions* by commanding Abraham to live a life of righteousness, integrity, morality, virtue, and justice. **This is the first contingency.**

***"As for me, behold, my covenant is with thee**, and thou shalt be a father of many nations." "I will establish (confirm and/or continue) my covenant as an everlasting covenant between me and you and your descendants after you **for the generations to come**, to be your God and the God of your descendants after you."* It is important for me to emphasize this point—*God* intended to make Abraham a "father of many nations"—not the father of many religions. Nor did *he* make him the father of the Arab and Israelite nations alone. *He* promised to multiply Abraham's seed to the extent they would establish, inhabit, and rule over many lands. Although, *God* specifically stated that he gave the land of Canaan to *all* the seed of Abraham for a perpetual habitation, he also inserted an amendment to this promise. The amendment made it clear that while the promise was an everlasting one; meaning *he* would never take it away from the seed of Abraham, *he* would confirm the Covenant with his descendants from one generation to the next, **to be their God and the God of their descendants.** In other words, *he* would visit the seed of Abraham from generation to generation to "confirm" they were abiding by the terms of the Covenant, and this one in particular—that *he* was their *God*, and the *God* of their children. The word, *establish,* may also be translated *"confirm."* Therefore, *he* not only made the Covenant reliant upon Abraham's seed living righteously, but also declared *his* will, *his* heart's desire—**<u>that He would continue to be the only God worshipped by Abraham's seed</u>**. The Hebrew Scriptures give us proof of this. When *God* visited the children of Israel and found they were worshipping other *gods*, he removed them from the land until they repented of their sin and returned to *him* in the sincerity of their hearts.

*God* repeats these words more than once; therefore, we must acknowledge the gravity of their importance **"... to be your God and the God of your descendants after you."** In addition, **"The whole land of Canaan,** where you are now an alien, *I will give as an everlasting possession to you and your descendants after you; <u>and I will be their God</u>*." **<u>This is the Second Contingency.</u>**

Before I go any further, let me give clarity to one issue. *God* made and sealed the Covenant with <u>Abraham</u>, no one else. The possession was Abraham's, and all the privileges and rights to the land were his. They only passed to his "seed," after his death. There are those who reject the notion that *God* excluded the unrighteous from any inheritance rights granted to the seed of Abraham. They claim the Israelites and/or Ishmaelites, are the legitimate descendants of their father by virtue of their ancestry alone, and are not bound by any contingencies. This is another strong *belief*, but the Covenant does not give credence to this position, nor is this *belief* sanctioned by the Torah or the Qur'an. Whoever disagrees with this position should produce their evidence for examination. However, if they base their "proofs" on hearsay or religious *beliefs:* they must be rejected. Personally, I require clear and decisive *evidence* showing that *God* modified the original Covenant with a decree that *anyone* who can certify that his lineage descends directly from Abraham is rightfully entitled to a portion of the land, whether or not he lives a righteous life acceptable to *God.* Now, if such evidence exists, and could be authenticated, all claims to the inerrancy of the Torah, Qur'an, and Bible would forever be invalidated. However, we all know there are no documents of this nature in existence.

*God*, who sees the future and calls what will take place many generations from now as though it is happening in the present, knew that Ishmael and Israel would have religious differences, and the nations Abraham fathered would be detached from one another. All the same, *he* promised the land – not only to the two brothers—but also to <u>all</u> the seed of Abraham, an issue I will address in more detail later in this book. Up to this point, there is more than enough evidence to support this statement—**"one's proof of genealogical descendancy is not sufficient to support a claim of entitlement or divine right to the land *God* promised to Abraham's seed."** The decisive requirement stressed in **the second contingency** is his loyalty to 'the Almighty *God* of Abraham', confirming that *he* is the only *God* they will worship. I am able to make this statement, having absolute confidence in its truthfulness, based on one condition alone; that the Palestinians and Israelis maintain their conviction that the writings of Moses are true and authentic. This is, was, and forever will be, the express desire of the Almighty:

*"Providing the seed of Abraham do not depart from the ways of the Lord, forsake the worship of the Almighty and turn to other gods, the land of Canaan is to be their perpetual habitation forever."*

For the record, Moses gave this account as to how he first became aware of a pre-existent Covenant. In the Biblical book of Exodus, Moses recalled a dialogue he had with the Lord after Pharaoh made life harsher for the Israelites. *"And Moses returned unto the LORD, and said, Lord, wherefore hast thou so evil entreated this people? Why is it that thou hast sent me? For since I came to Pharaoh to speak in thy name, he hath done evil to this people; neither hast thou delivered thy people at all."* (Ex. 5.22,23 emphasis added)

> ¹Then the LORD said unto Moses, Now shalt thou see what I will do to Pharaoh: for with a strong hand shall he let them go, and with a strong hand shall he drive them out of his land.
> ²And *God* spake unto Moses, and said unto him, I am **the LORD**:
>
> [**YHWH**, the ineffable name, (explanation and emphasis added)]
>
> ³And I appeared unto Abraham, unto Isaac, and unto Jacob, by the **name of *God Almighty***, but by my **name *JEHOVAH*** was I not known to them.
> *⁴And I have also established my covenant with them, to give them the land of Canaan, the land of their pilgrimage, wherein they were strangers.*
> ⁵And I have also heard the groaning of the children of Israel, whom the Egyptians keep in bondage; and I have remembered my covenant. (Ex. 6.1-5 italics and emphasis added)

Getting back to the subject in question: Abraham had only fathered Ishmael during the period the Covenant was entered into. In fact, *God*, made this promise to all the seed of Abraham before *he* told Abraham that Sarah would bear him another son. However, I want to address **the third contingency in the Covenant** before I get involved in this issue, which will give additional credence to my earlier statements:

> ⁹And *God* said unto Abraham, Thou shalt keep my covenant therefore, thou, and thy seed after thee in their generations.
> ¹⁰This is my covenant, which ye shall keep, between me and you and thy seed after thee; Every man child among you shall be circumcised.
> ¹¹And ye shall circumcise the flesh of your foreskin; and it shall be a token of the covenant betwixt me and you.
> ¹²And he that is eight days old shall be circumcised among you, every man child in your generations, he that is born in the house, or bought with money of any stranger, which is not of thy seed.
> ¹³He that is born in thy house, and he that is bought with thy money, must needs be circumcised: <u>and my covenant shall be in your flesh for an everlasting covenant.</u>
> ¹⁴And the uncircumcised man child whose flesh of his foreskin is not circumcised, that soul shall be cut off from his people; he hath broken my covenant. (Gen. 17. 9-14)

The Covenant was more than just an instrument that made provision for the perpetual home of Abraham's seed. It contained a solemn oath, a commitment, with bonds as strong as a marriage, between Abraham, his seed, and *God*. It was customary for all parties to exchange something of value when sealing the terms of a covenant. For example: if two people entered into an agreement to transfer a parcel of real estate, the owner would agree to surrender the land conditioned upon the purchaser giving up something of equal value, such as a certain amount of money or other consideration in trade. In like manner, *God* offered to make a perpetual covenant with Abraham and his seed to give them *his* love, protection, and salvation from generation to generation. What did *he* ask for in return? The immediate answer here is the circumcision of all the seed of Abraham. In the literal sense, this is true. Like all covenants initiated by *God*, they were sealed by drops of blood. Why blood? Some, in their ignorance of *God*, have said things like; "The *God* of the Hebrews is a bloodthirsty *God* who enjoys seeing his people spill their blood." This is an outrageously absurd statement.

*God's* desire is for everyone to know that all vows and commitments to *him* are lifetime obligations, enduring pledges, and not shallow offerings of empty words. With the shedding of a small amount of blood, and a piece of his flesh, the covenant maker "acknowledged" he understood the gravity of the agreement, that it was a life commitment, an unbreakable pledge that he must fulfill and pass on to his children and grandchildren as well. Therefore, the blood represented more than just a seal of approval. In fact, Moses gave us the answer when he said, *"... what doth the LORD thy God require of thee, but to fear the LORD thy God, to walk in all his ways, and to love him, and to serve the LORD thy God with all thy heart and with all thy soul. To keep the commandments of the LORD, and his statutes, which I command thee this day for thy good?"* (Deut. 10.12, 13 emphasis added)

Nothing in this statement indicated that *God* was demanding the sacrificial blood of *his* people. This verse summed up the intended meaning of all the contingencies in the Covenant, a life of righteous living and devotion to the "One True *God*". After all, what can a man give to *God* of equal value in exchange for life? All the silver, gold, and natural resources belong to *him* already, including the cattle and livestock on a thousand hills. The one sacrifice and present *God* wants is the willful offering of a man's most valuable assets, his life, undivided love, and devotion; or simply put, "life for life". *He* said to Moses, *"For the life of the flesh is in the blood."* (Lev. 17.11 emphasis added) Having said this, let us return to the Covenant.

> [15] *God* also said to Abraham, "As for Sarai your wife, you are no longer to call her Sarai; her name will be Sarah.
> [16] I will bless her and will surely give you a son by her. I will bless her so that she will be the mother of nations; kings of peoples will come from her."
> [17] Abraham fell facedown; he laughed and said to himself, "Will a son be born to a man a hundred years old? Will Sarah bear a child at the age of ninety?"
> **[18] And Abraham said to *God*, "If only Ishmael might live under your blessing!"**
> [19] Then *God* said, "Yes, but your wife Sarah will bear you a son, and you will call him Isaac. I will establish my covenant with him as an everlasting covenant for his descendants after him. (Gen.17.15-19 emphasis added)

*"I will establish my covenant with him* (Sarah's son) *as an everlasting covenant for his descendants after him."* There

were two good reasons for *God* to repeat *his* promise and include Isaac's name the second time. The Scripture does not indicate this and therefore the reader should deem this an opinion; but considering the history of the religions and the doctrines perpetuated over hundreds of centuries, there is ample evidence to support my *opinion*. To begin with, *God* foresaw the disparaging statements the Ishmaelites would circulate in an attempt to exclude Isaac from their inheritance because *God* used the term "seed" which they interpreted as meaning one (singular). Therefore, the *All Knowing God* decided it would be prudent to repeat the promise and include Isaac's name. Secondly, Ishmael's descendants would certainly make the argument that when Abraham said to *God, "If only Ishmael might live under your blessing!"* Abraham, himself, believed *God* made this promise with only Ishmael in mind because he could not imagine himself becoming a father again. Of course, this would give strength to the first argument.

What was this Covenant of promise *God* made with Isaac **"for"** his descendants after him? I am aware of the scope and nature of this Covenant; but it would not be wise for me to reveal it in this writing because it would become a matter of contention and defeat the purpose intended. *God* will manifest the need for the fulfillment of this Covenant in *his* time, after a lasting peace becomes a reality, and at a time that Wisdom and Prudence deem appropriate.

In this book, I am giving my utmost attention to Abraham's Covenant with *God* and the solution it provides for a lasting peace between the brothers, nothing more. To reveal the essence of the Covenant with Isaac is pointless anyway, as it will not alter or change Abraham's Covenant one iota. The Covenant will continue uninterrupted forever as long as the sons of Abraham maintain a sincere devotion to the True and Living *God* out of the integrity of their hearts, not out of fear of retribution or banishment.

*"And as for Ishmael, I have heard you: I will surely bless him; I will make him fruitful and will greatly increase his numbers. He will be the father of twelve princes, and I will make him into a great nation."* (Gen. 17.20 NIV)

It is apparent from the passage that Ishmael <u>was included in the Covenant,</u> subject to all the conditions contained therein. If simply mentioning Ishmael by name was enough to give his descendants "standing," then Isaac's descendants would have the same standing, and the issue should be resolved. Unfortunately, that is not sufficient because their standing, or ability to make a claim, was not determined by genealogy, but by devotion and loyalty to the one true *God*. Can either of them make a case for entitlement based on their compliance with the three contingencies in the Covenant?

Whether the identity of the Covenant maker, or *Testator*, is *God*, as *he* introduced *himself*, or an angel speaking on behalf of *God*, is irrelevant. The fact remains, nothing of any significance has presented itself to make a legitimate challenge to the words of the "Voice," the *One* who made the Covenant with Abraham and then revealed it to Moses. Nonetheless, we still do not have *absolute proof* that it was the same *God, Lord,* or *angel that* appeared to Abraham and Moses.

## *SEPARATION OF THE SONS*

The evidence presented in the Biblical narratives will confirm my assertion that the separation of Abraham's sons was not the result of a direct act of hostility or aggression by one brother against the other; nor was it an act that can be attributable to *God* or Abraham. Certain individuals caused the resentments that separated them and resulted in a division they never wanted. Let us take a closer look at the Mosaic account of the relationship between Isaac and Ishmael. As previously stated, Sarah was unable to bear children; therefore, she decided to use her slave girl, Hagar, as a surrogate mother. *"And he went in unto Hagar, and she conceived: and when she saw that she had conceived her mistress was despised in her eyes. And Sarah said unto Abram, "My wrong be upon thee: I have given my maid into thy bosom; and when she saw that she had conceived, I was despised in her eyes: the LORD judge between me and thee."* But, Abram said unto Sarah, *"Behold, thy maid is in thy hand; do to her as it pleaseth thee."* And when Sarah dealt hardly with her, she fled from her face. (Gen. 16. 4-6 quotations added)

We can make a few intelligent deductions, and offer a few good opinions here; however, as I have stated several times, it is my intent to stick to the actual statements. We have enough information to make the following assertions: Sarah was despondent over not bearing children; She felt that her slave girl looked at her with the same contempt she had endured throughout her childbearing years; and further came to believe that her decision to have children by Hagar worsened her status.

The statement, *"May the Lord judge between you and me"* is a petition of sorts whereby one asks the Lord to judge between the integrity of their heart, and that of another's. It appears that Sarah needed some reassurance that Abraham did not share the same contempt for her as Hagar. When Abraham told her to do with her as she wished, he was informing her that nothing had changed between them; that Hagar had no more importance or distinction than before she became pregnant, and that Sarah retained her eminence in his heart. When Sarah treated Hagar harshly, she ran away. The story continues with an angel of the Lord discovering Hagar by a fountain, or well. The Lord had dispatched the angel to bring her a message from *his* own heart and mouth.

> ⁷And the angel of the LORD found her by a fountain of water in the wilderness, by the fountain in the way to Shur.
> ⁸And he said, Hagar, Sarah's maid, whence camest thou? and whither wilt thou go? And she said, I flee from the face of my mistress Sarah.
> ⁹And the angel of the LORD said unto her, Return to thy mistress, and submit thyself under her hands.
> **¹⁰And the angel of the LORD said unto her, I will multiply thy seed exceedingly, that it shall not be numbered for multitude.**
> ¹¹And **the angel** of the LORD **said** unto her, Behold, **thou art with child, and shalt bear a son, and shalt call his name Ishmael**; because the LORD hath heard thy affliction.

¹²And he will be a wild man; his hand will be against every man, and every man's hand against him; and he shall dwell in the presence of all his brethren. (Gen. 16.7-12 Sarai renamed)

What can we glean from this testimony? First, and foremost, **it was <u>Sarah</u>, not Abraham, and certainly not the Lord, who wanted Hagar to leave and take Ishmael with her.** A dejected Hagar was bearing Abraham's son, which was important enough to the Lord to send *his* angel to find her, comfort her, and tell her to return home and submit to Sarah's authority. Then he delivered the message that would give her new hope: *"I will multiply thy seed exceedingly, that it shall not be numbered for multitude."*

*God* pronounced a blessing upon Ishmael while he was still in his mother's womb, before he had a chance to do good or evil, and before he had a chance to know *God* or reject *him*. *God*, knowing in advance the direction Ishmael would take in life, blessed him before Hagar gave birth. All three religions have already resolved the question stating the Lord would never bless an idol-worshipper. Therefore, we must conclude that Ishmael met *God's* approval for a blessing, and *he* knew Ishmael would teach his children to love, serve, and honour the Living *God*, as his father did, in order to bring the blessings *God* promised upon his seed for the generations to come. (Those who hold fast to the doctrines of predestination, pre-selection, and the sovereignty of *God*, should not have any difficulty with this passage, but unfortunately, that is not the case.)

The angel also told her the name Abraham would give the child, **Ishmael.** *God* gave the lad his name—not his mother or father—a name that had a special meaning: *"God* has heard your affliction." *God,* whose name and reputation is rooted in Mercy, looked upon her misery, heard her groans, and had compassion on her and the child. *He* gave her the hope that she would become the mother of an innumerable people. Embracing this newfound hope, which *God* would never give and then disappoint, Hagar returned to her mistress as commanded.

Some twelve or thirteen years later, Sarah gave birth to Isaac. As was customary, the family threw a party for the child to celebrate his being weaned from the breast. It was at this party the envy of Sarah revealed itself again:

> ⁹And Sarah saw the son of Hagar the Egyptian, which she had born unto Abraham, mocking.
> ¹⁰Wherefore she said unto Abraham, Cast out this bondwoman and her son: for the son of this bondwoman shall not be heir with my son, even with Isaac.
> ¹¹And the thing was very grievous in Abraham's sight because of his son.
> ¹²And *God* said unto Abraham, Let it not be grievous in thy sight because of the lad, and because of thy bondwoman; in all that Sarah hath said unto thee, hearken unto her voice; for in Isaac shall thy seed be called.
> **¹³And also of the son of the bondwoman will I make a nation, because he is thy seed.**

¹⁴And Abraham rose up early in the morning, and took bread, and a bottle of water, and gave it unto Hagar, putting it on her shoulder, and the child, and sent her away: and she departed, and wandered in the wilderness of Beersheba.
¹⁵And the water was spent in the bottle, and she cast the child under one of the shrubs.
¹⁶And she went, and sat her down over against him a good way off, as it were a bowshot: for she said, let me not see the death of the child. And she sat over against him, and lift up her voice, and wept.
¹⁷And **God heard the voice of the lad**; and the angel of *God* called to Hagar out of heaven, and said unto her, **what aileth thee, Hagar? fear not; for *God* hath heard the voice of the lad where he is.**
¹⁸Arise, lift up the lad, and hold him in thine hand; for I will make him a great nation.
¹⁹ And *God* opened her eyes, and she saw a well of water; and she went, and filled the bottle with water, and gave the lad drink.
²⁰**And *God* was with the lad;** and he grew, and dwelt in the wilderness, and became an archer.
²¹And he dwelt in the wilderness of Paran: and his mother took him a wife out of the land of Egypt. (Gen. 21.9-21 emphasis added)

Perhaps Hagar was too grieved to pray; or she felt abandoned, even by *God*. The text does not give us these answers. However, we can answer this question: does *God* hear the prayers of sinners? Yes, when they cry out for forgiveness with a repentant heart; but Ishmael was not repenting! From these words, I am able to conclude that *God* did not consider the boy a sinner or an idolater. I can find nothing in them that remotely indicates *God* rejected Ishmael. Secondly, despite the fact that Abraham sent his son away, we can clearly see by his grief that this was not an easy decision, for they had a very close father and son relationship.

**Sarah was the one who intentionally brought about the separation between the brothers.** Isaac was much too young to have made that decision. Ishmael was by now fifteen or sixteen years of age and he certainly did not want to separate from his family. Where would he have gone? What was his crime—mocking his brother? Was he actually "mocking" his infant brother as Sarah stated? The Hebrew word indicates that while the word in question may be translated *mocking*; it also means to *laugh aloud* and to *sport with*. Was he laughing at the boy in a mocking way, or was he sporting with him? Interestingly, this is the same word used in the following Scripture: *"And it came to pass, when he (Isaac) had been there a long time, that Abimelech king of the Philistines looked out at a window, and saw, and, behold, Isaac was **sporting with** Rebekah his wife."* (Gen. 26.8) This was the same word previously translated, *mocking*. Was Isaac mocking his wife, or was he being playful with her? Apparently, his "playfulness" was endearing enough to convince Abimelech she was his wife.

There are a few possibilities that may explain why Sarah was so intent on ridding herself of Hagar and her son. For example, it is possible she was uncomfortable with Ishmael expressing too much affection toward his brother and she was adamantly against them being close. Perhaps, after Isaac was born, she denied Ishmael's legitimacy and regarded him as an "illegitimate" son. We can only guess since nothing is written. However, if Ishmael was scornful toward his brother, would banishing a teenager from his family be an appropriate punishment? I do not think so. However, the one thing we do know for sure is that *Sarah was the one behind his expulsion, no one else!* The second thing we know for sure is this—she was very emphatic when she said that Ishmael *would not be a joint inheritor with her son.*

Ishmael awoke, as he had done every other day of his life, to a loving and *God*-fearing family. However, this day would be the most traumatic of his life. He was accused of something he did not do. He was shocked to discover that he was being sent into the wilderness, accompanied only by his mother. He could not remain on the land, could not return to his home, nor would his younger brother grow up with him. There is no doubt Ishmael was devastated. Why did Sarah hate him so much? He grew up calling her his mother. Tears were flowing down Abraham's face. Isaac was probably screaming for his brother. Why was his father submitting to the will of Sarah, when it was obvious he did not want to send him away? Now, he was to be denied his father's love, protection, guidance, and future stake in the only land he knew. Why, what had he done?

He would relate the devastation he felt on the worst day of his life to his children and grandchildren until his death. Was he aware he was implanting the emotionally charged "triggers" that would affect their behaviors throughout their generations?

Did Ishmael disappear? Did Isaac lose contact with his brother? The Scripture tells us that both sons buried their father. Someone thought enough about Ishmael to get him the message. Was it Isaac?

## *CONTRADICTION or MISTRANSLATION*

During the time that elapsed between the 21$^{st}$ and 22$^{nd}$ chapters of the Biblical book of Genesis, a different story seemed to evolve. From these verses, many would be led to believe that *God* eliminated the name of Ishmael altogether. Here is the Scripture to which I am referring —

*"And it came to pass after these things that God did tempt Abraham, and said unto him, 'Abraham': and he said, 'Behold, here I am.' And he said,* **'Take now thy son, thine only son Isaac, whom thou lovest,** *and get thee into the land of Moriah; and offer him there for a burnt offering upon one of the mountains which I will tell thee of.'"*
(Gen. 22.1,2 quotations and emphasis added)

Moses reported that *God, the* "Voice" he had come to recognize, told Abraham to take his **only son** up to Moriah. Suddenly, numerous questions filled my mind. To say that I was in a quandary is an understatement. "Could this be the same *God?*" I wondered. Why would *he* say "your *only* son?" Did Moses or his scribes misstate *his* words? If not, then either the "Voice" erred in *his* speech or, *this God,* this "Voice," is a different Persona. What happened to Ishmael? Muslims, Jews, and Christians believe whole-heartedly that *God* is perfect in Wisdom, and it is impossible for *him* to err in speech or action.

Yet, I have to admit I was troubled. I knew that if the Lord did not show me *his* truth, I could not continue with this work. It would be impossible to substantiate the claim that the *God* who identified himself to Moses, the "Voice" he came to recognize, was the same "Voice" that revealed the terms of the Covenant to him. In a sense, I am giving you some insight into how I was taught to think, to question every word, and to continue searching until I was left with nothing but Truth.

I searched several translations of the Hebrew and Christian Scriptures. They also translated these words the same way, "Take your son, your only *son* Isaac, whom you love..." The Muslim position holds that Abraham took Ishmael, instead of Isaac, up to the mountain of sacrifice. Nevertheless, if the *Voice* had said, "Take your only *son* Ishmael...," what difference would it make? Ishmael was not Abraham's only son anymore than Isaac was!

When I recalled *God's* conditions for the execution of *his* promises, there were only three reasons, aside from the "Voice" being a different entity altogether, by which *God* would have eliminated one of them, or blotted out their name from under heaven — that of **turning away from living an upright life, worshipping other gods, or failing to circumcise their children.** Any of these would have constituted a breach of the Covenant. If this happened, another distinctive characteristic of *God* comes to mind. Would *God* demand that every judge administer justice impartially, without regard to a person's title or position, and then expose *his* own bias and prejudice toward an accused? According to the Torah and the prophets, *God* **always** gave clear warnings to Israel when they were going astray and sent prophets to preach repentance. Did *he* refuse to send a warning to Ishmael? Did someone write in any of the known Scriptures that *God* sent a prophet to the Ishmaelites and they refused to change their ways? Yes?

Who wrote it? Which book can I find it in? Moreover, if it is written, I would need a second witness to validate the testimony. It is easy for someone to make a claim that Ishmael or Isaac turned to other *god*s, but there is not one shred of written evidence in this section of the narrative to corroborate that statement. Anyone can "preach" or write their opinion, but proving it is another matter. If the testimony is not in writing, then we are only guessing, or providing a "holy opinion" of the truth, whatever that is.

I have heard devout believers give the following response when they thought someone was challenging *God's* actions or integrity. "*God* can do anything he wants; *he's God!* No, that is a lie right out of Hell! *God* **cannot** present *himself* as unrighteous in judgment unless that is *his* nature! It is **not possible** for *him* to display or promote the sin of bias or prejudice and retain *his* crown and reputation for Perfection and Holiness. If *God can do anything*, are we also saying *he* has the potential to **lie, steal, and make himself unholy or unrighteous**? I can assure you I would never be swayed; and furthermore, I would emphatically declare, "No! It is impossible for *God* to sin!"

Luke, the author of the New Testament book of Acts, states that *God* rebuked Peter, an apostle of Jesus and one highly revered in Christianity, in a vision because of his prejudice against Gentiles. Peter held the Roman's in disdain and refused to minister to them. Why did *God* rebuke him? Because prejudice is a form of pride, an evil in the sight of *God*, because an individual portrays himself or herself as better than, or more esteemed than, someone else. Could *God* be guilty of pride? Never!

Something is amiss here. Nothing adds up. I cannot discern the presence or character of the *God* of Mercy in this Scripture. *God* is perfect; and being perfect, he cannot change! I have come to <u>know</u> this, not merely believe it! If Ishmael was guilty of fornication or idolatry, the *God* I have come to know would have caused him to suffer the same maladies any other people, including Israel, suffered. Furthermore, if his name was "blotted out" of the Book of Life as some contend: it would not have happened before *God* gave him chances to repent and turn back to the True and Living *God* just as *he* gave Israel and the rest of us many opportunities to do.

Before I gave in to what appeared to be a hopeless dead end, and after much prayer, the Lord put a thought in my mind to find out if the verse could have been translated incorrectly. In the King James Version of the Bible, the words "only *son*" appears three times. The word translated "**only**" came from the Hebrew word, *Yachiyd*. The word, *son,* is in italics. Every student of the Scriptures learns that it was common for the translators to place a word in italics to indicate it was **not part of the original text** but they added it to *"simplify translation".* **'Take now thy son, <u>thine only --- Isaac</u>, whom thou lovest,** doesn't appear to have originated with a *God* who is perfect in wisdom and knowledge because it didn't make sense. As I searched a little deeper, I discovered that the word *Yachiyd* is also translated **Beloved in** Hebrew. There was the answer to the truth I was seeking! The translators could have easily translated the verse as, *"***Take now thy son, thy <u>beloved</u> Isaac, whom thou lovest....***"*

Or, in the Muslim tradition, the verse should have read, ***Take now thy son, thy <u>beloved</u> Ishmael, whom thou lovest....***"

Had the scribes employed this translation, there would have been no debate on the subject. This statement would be consistent with others made by the "Voice" and would not have given rise to any of the scorn and ridicule the agnostics enjoy inflicting on the devout who are unable to respond with *God's* truth. The question I present is this, who stood to gain by mistranslating this verse? Was it an accident? If the translators were aware of the attributes of *God*, or at least considered them, they would have known their translation created a distinct flaw in the persona of *God* that tarnished *his* infallibility, omniscient qualities, and purity. I have a suspicion this was a decision made with the counsel of others who, knowing the truth, conspired to withhold it from the children of Israel, and/or the children of Ishmael; but unfortunately, I have no way to prove it.

With the resolution of this issue, everything falls into place. I have thoroughly examined the Covenant and all of its elements, and I can bear witness to the following:

• I cannot find any inconsistencies in the words of "the Voice" that conversed with Moses. To debate whether the verse I questioned is a mistranslation, or was accurately translated is ludicrous. If the clergy *chooses to believe* the verse is translated properly; so be it. The proper translation allows me to confirm the identity of the Testator, and does not change the stipulations contained in the Covenant in any way; detract from, or obscure the words and intent of the Testator, nor compromises or eliminates any of the named heirs, or negates the obligations they must fulfill.

• The presence of the divine nature of the *angel*, *God*, or *Lord*, I affectionately identify in this book as the "Voice", *is evident. His* words are consistent with other statements and deeds attributable to the "Voice", and have the same distinctive characteristics and qualities consistent with Truth, as Moses declared them.

• *God* gave Abraham, his sons, Isaac and Ishmael, and their seed, the right to inhabit the land of Canaan perpetually, conditioned upon their fulfillment of the three contingencies named in the Covenant. Their dedication to the terms of the Covenant is what entitles them to their portion of the inheritance.

• None of the sons of Abraham— Ishmael, Isaac, nor any of their descendants, can validate the claim that only **one son** is the "sole and rightful heir to Abraham's estate" and be in accord with the stipulations contained in the Covenant.

• I am certain of this one affirmation. When *God* entered into the Covenant with Abraham, it was, still is, and forever will be, *his* will to fulfill this promise to him and his seed—

*"**The whole land of Canaan**, where you are now an alien, I will give as an everlasting possession <u>to you</u> and <u>your descendants after you</u>; and <u>**I will be their God.**</u>"*

## *RECONCILIATION OF THE BROTHERS*

There is a story in the Hebrew Bible I want to include in this book. A good friend of mine, who is very knowledgeable in Islamic culture and the Quran, has advised me there is some disagreement among Jewish and Muslim scholars as to its authenticity, and in particular to one of the persons noted in the story, *Esau*. He also advised me that none of the Arabic families count their descent from Esau and to raise this issue may be problematic for many.

Whoever authored this tale is not of importance to me, and in deference to the debate over its legitimacy, I am not debating whether it is genuine or not. However, my position of only presenting Truth raises a question I feel obliged to address. Why would I insist on including a story whose credibility is in question? I am basing the inclusion of this story on one premise alone; this tale, or legend, reveals an inspiring example of how *God* brought about a monumental reconciliation between two brothers, one of whom held a deep hatred for the other. The author's knowledge of the *Godly* principles of forgiveness and reconciliation is evident in his artistic depiction of the righteous attributes one must possess in order to resolve a bitter conflict. Moses incorporates this tale in the book we identify with as the Biblical book of Genesis.

According to the author, Isaac and Rebekah had a set of fraternal twins, Esau the elder, and Jacob the second-born. The boys lived with their parents in the same land for over forty years until something happened that would strain their emotional ties and change their lives for many years to come. In the storyline, Isaac lost his vision due to age. In anticipation of his death, he called his firstborn son, Esau, and asked him to go out and catch some venison and prepare it the way he liked it; afterwards, he would give him the "blessing of the firstborn." Prior to this series of events, the author details an arrangement agreed to between the brothers in which Esau allegedly "sold" his birthright to Jacob for a morsel of food. He never tells us if Isaac was aware of this exchange, or if he had dismissed it as childish foolishness. Apparently, Rebekah overheard the exchange between Isaac and Esau and executed what may have been a pre-conceived plan she had contrived years before. This story clearly establishes the fact that it was Rebekah, not Jacob, who devised the scheme. Here is the narrative:

> [5]And Rebekah heard when Isaac spake to Esau his son. And Esau went to the field to hunt for venison, and to bring it.
> [6]And Rebekah spake unto Jacob her son, saying, Behold, I heard thy father speak unto Esau thy brother, saying,
> [7]Bring me venison, and make me savoury meat, that I may eat, and bless thee before the LORD before my death.
> [8]Now therefore, my son, obey my voice according to that which I command thee.
> [9]Go now to the flock, and fetch me from thence two good kids of the goats; and I will make them savoury meat for thy father, such as he loveth:

¹⁰And thou shalt bring it to thy father, that he may eat, and that he may bless thee before his death.

¹¹And Jacob said to Rebekah his mother, Behold, Esau my brother is a hairy man, and I am a smooth man:

¹²My father peradventure will feel me, and I shall seem to him as a deceiver; and I shall bring a curse upon me, and not a blessing.

¹³And his mother said unto him, Upon me be thy curse, my son: only obey my voice, and go fetch me them.

¹⁴And he went, and fetched, and brought them to his mother: and his mother made savoury meat, such as his father loved.

¹⁵And Rebekah took goodly raiment of her eldest son Esau, which were with her in the house, and put them upon Jacob her younger son:

¹⁶And she put the skins of the kids of the goats upon his hands, and upon the smooth of his neck:

¹⁷And she gave the savoury meat and the bread, which she had prepared, into the hand of her son Jacob.

¹⁸And he came unto his father, and said, My father: and he said, Here am I; who art thou, my son?

¹⁹And Jacob said unto his father, I am Esau thy firstborn; I have done according as thou badest me: arise, I pray thee, sit and eat of my venison, that thy soul may bless me.

²⁰And Isaac said unto his son, How is it that thou hast found it so quickly, my son? And he said, Because the LORD thy *God* brought it to me.

²¹And Isaac said unto Jacob, Come near, I pray thee, that I may feel thee, my son, whether thou be my very son Esau or not.

²²And Jacob went near unto Isaac his father; and he felt him, and said, The voice is Jacob's voice, but the hands are the hands of Esau.

²³And he discerned him not, because his hands were hairy, as his brother Esau's hands: so he blessed him.

²⁴And he said, Art thou my very son Esau? And he said, I am.

²⁵And he said, Bring it near to me, and I will eat of my son's venison, that my soul may bless thee. And he brought it near to him, and he did eat: and he brought him wine, and he drank.

²⁶And his father Isaac said unto him, Come near now, and kiss me, my son.

²⁷And he came near, and kissed him: and he smelled the smell of his raiment, and blessed him, and said, See, the smell of my son is as the smell of a field which the LORD hath blessed:

²⁸Therefore *God* give thee of the dew of heaven, and the fatness of the earth, and plenty of corn and wine:

²⁹Let people serve thee, and nations bow down to thee: be lord over thy brethren, and let thy mother's sons bow down to thee: cursed be every

one that curseth thee, and blessed be he that blesseth thee.

³⁰And it came to pass, as soon as Isaac had made an end of blessing Jacob, and Jacob was yet scarce gone out from the presence of Isaac his father, that Esau his brother came in from his hunting.

³¹And he also had made savoury meat, and brought it unto his father, and said unto his father, Let my father arise, and eat of his son's venison, that thy soul may bless me.

³²And Isaac his father said unto him, Who art thou? And he said, I am thy son, thy firstborn Esau.

³³And Isaac trembled very exceedingly, and said, Who? Where is he that hath taken venison, and brought it me, and I have eaten of all before thou camest, and have blessed him? yea, and he shall be blessed.

³⁴And when Esau heard the words of his father, he cried with a great and exceeding bitter cry, and said unto his father, Bless me, even me also, O my father.

³⁵And he said, Thy brother came with subtlety, and hath taken away thy blessing.

³⁶And he said, Is not he rightly named Jacob? for he hath supplanted me these two times: he took away my birthright; and, behold, now he hath taken away my blessing. And he said, Hast thou not reserved a blessing for me?

>³⁷And Isaac answered and said unto Esau, Behold, I have made him thy lord, and all his brethren have I given to him for servants; and with corn and wine have I sustained him: and what shall I do now unto thee, my son?
>
>³⁸And Esau said unto his father, Hast thou but one blessing, my father? bless me, even me also, O my father. And Esau lifted up his voice, and wept.
>
>³⁹And Isaac his father answered and said unto him, Behold, thy dwelling shall be the fatness of the earth, and of the dew of heaven from above;
>
>⁴⁰And by thy sword shalt thou live, and shalt serve thy brother; and it shall come to pass when thou shalt have the dominion, that thou shalt break his yoke from off thy neck (Gen. 27. 5-40)

In another version, the word, "dominion" is translated, "breaks loose". Whether it means, "breaks loose" or "dominion" is insignificant in comparison to the importance of the statement, or prophecy, Isaac made on behalf of Esau. *"Esau hated Jacob because of the blessing wherewith his father blessed him: and Esau said in his heart, 'the days of mourning for my father are at hand; then will I slay my brother Jacob.'"* (Gen. 27.41 quotations added) Jacob had robbed him of a blessing to which he felt entitled. Because of this, hatred filled his heart for Jacob from that moment, and he began to plot how and when he would kill him. No doubt, his plan would have succeeded if he had not revealed it to a "confidant" who exposed the plan to Rebekah:

⁴²And these words of Esau her elder son were told to Rebekah: and she sent and called Jacob her younger son, and said unto him, Behold, thy brother Esau, as touching thee, doth comfort himself, purposing to kill thee.

⁴³Now therefore, my son, obey my voice; and arise, flee thou to Laban my brother to Haran;

⁴⁴And tarry with him a few days, until thy brother's fury turn away;

⁴⁵Until thy brother's anger turn away from thee, and he forget that which thou hast done to him: then I will send, and fetch thee from thence: why should I be deprived also of you both in one day? (Gen. 27.42-45)

¹And Isaac called Jacob, and blessed him, and charged him, and said unto him, Thou shalt not take a wife of the daughters of Canaan.

²Arise, go to Padanaram, to the house of Bethuel thy mother's father; and take thee a wife from thence of the daughters of Laban thy mother's brother.

³And *God* Almighty bless thee, and make thee fruitful, and multiply thee, that thou mayest be a multitude of people;

⁴And give thee the blessing of Abraham, to thee, and to thy seed with thee; that thou mayest inherit the land wherein thou art a stranger, which *God* gave unto Abraham.

> ⁵And Isaac sent away Jacob: and he went to Padanaram unto Laban, son of Bethuel the Syrian, the brother of Rebekah, Jacob's and Esau's mother. (Gen. 28.1-5)

Jacob would soon learn the agony and emotional strain that deception brings. He had made an agreement to serve Laban for seven years so that he might marry his daughter, Rachel. However, on their wedding night, Laban substituted his daughter, Leah, in place of her younger sister. In the morning, Jacob discovered the ruse and was enraged, "Why did you deceive me?" he screamed. Perhaps he needed this experience to relate to the disappointment and distrust his own acts of deception fostered.

After fulfilling Leah's week, Laban gave him Rachel, after Jacob agreed to serve him for an additional seven years. Altogether, Jacob remained in Padan-Aram for twenty years, serving fourteen years for his wives and six more for his cattle. At the end of that period, Jacob had a vision in which the Lord told him to return to the land of his kindred.

Was twenty years enough time for the anger of Esau to soften? According to the narrator, Jacob was hopeful, but unsure. Nevertheless, in obedience to the vision, he gathered his family and belongings and began the trip back. As he travelled, he devised a plan on how he might appease his brother's anger. He decided that if he sent messengers to Esau in advance of his return and offer to share his wealth with him, Esau might receive him favorably.

³And Jacob sent messengers before him to Esau his brother unto the land of Seir, the country of Edom.

⁴And he commanded them, saying, Thus shall ye speak unto my lord Esau; Thy servant Jacob saith thus, I have sojourned with Laban, and stayed there until now:

⁵And I have oxen, and asses, flocks, and menservants, and womenservants: and I have sent to tell my lord, that I may find grace in thy sight.

⁶And the messengers returned to Jacob, saying, We came to thy brother Esau, and also he cometh to meet thee, and four hundred men with him.

⁷Then Jacob was greatly afraid and distressed: and he divided the people that was with him, and the flocks, and herds, and the camels, into two bands;

⁸And said, If Esau come to the one company, and smite it, then the other company which is left shall escape.

⁹And Jacob said, O *God* of my father Abraham, and *God* of my father Isaac, the LORD which saidst unto me, Return unto thy country, and to thy kindred, and I will deal well with thee:

¹⁰I am not worthy of the least of all the mercies, and of all the truth, which thou hast showed unto thy servant; for with my staff I passed over this Jordan; and now I am become two bands.

¹¹Deliver me, I pray thee, from the hand of my brother, from the hand of Esau: for I fear him, lest he will come and smite me, and the mother with the children.

¹²And thou saidst, I will surely do thee good, and make thy seed as the sand of the sea, which cannot be numbered for multitude.

¹³And he lodged there that same night; and took of that which came to his hand a present for Esau his brother;

¹⁴Two hundred she goats, and twenty he goats, two hundred ewes, and twenty rams,

¹⁵Thirty milch camels with their colts, forty kine, and ten bulls, twenty she asses, and ten foals.

¹⁶And he delivered them into the hand of his servants, every drove by themselves; and said unto his servants, Pass over before me, and put a space betwixt drove and drove.

¹⁷And he commanded the foremost, saying, When Esau my brother meeteth thee, and asketh thee, saying, Whose art thou? and whither goest thou? and whose are these before thee?

¹⁸Then thou shalt say, They be thy servant Jacob's; it is a present sent unto my lord Esau: and, behold, also he is behind us.

¹⁹And so commanded he the second, and the third, and all that followed the droves, saying, On this manner shall ye speak unto Esau, when ye find him.

$^{20}$And say ye moreover, Behold, thy servant Jacob is behind us. For he said, I will appease him with the present that goeth before me, and afterward I will see his face; peradventure he will accept of me. (Gen. 32.3-20)

$^{1}$And Jacob lifted up his eyes, and looked, and, behold, Esau came, and with him four hundred men. And he divided the children unto Leah, and unto Rachel, and unto the two handmaids.
$^{2}$And he put the handmaids and their children foremost, and Leah and her children after, and Rachel and Joseph hindermost.
$^{3}$And he passed over before them, and bowed himself to the ground seven times, until he came near to his brother.
$^{4}$And Esau ran to meet him, and embraced him, and fell on his neck, and kissed him: and they wept.
$^{5}$And he lifted up his eyes, and saw the women and the children; and said, Who are those with thee? And he said, The children which *God* hath graciously given thy servant.
$^{6}$Then the handmaidens came near, they and their children, and they bowed themselves.
$^{7}$And Leah also with her children came near, and bowed themselves: and after came Joseph near and Rachel, and they bowed themselves.

⁸And he said, What meanest thou by all this drove which I met? And he said, These are to find grace in the sight of my lord.

⁹And Esau said, I have enough, my brother; keep that thou hast unto thyself.

¹⁰And Jacob said, Nay, I pray thee, if now I have found grace in thy sight, then receive my present at my hand: for therefore I have seen thy face, as though I had seen the face of *God*, and thou wast pleased with me.

¹¹Take, I pray thee, my blessing that is brought to thee; because *God* hath dealt graciously with me, and because I have enough. And he urged him, and he took it.

¹²And he said, Let us take our journey, and let us go, and I will go before thee.

¹³And he said unto him, My lord knoweth that the children are tender, and the flocks and herds with young are with me: and if men should overdrive them one day, all the flock will die.

¹⁴Let my lord, I pray thee, pass over before his servant: and I will lead on softly, according as the cattle that goeth before me and the children be able to endure, until I come unto my lord unto Seir.

¹⁵And Esau said, Let me now leave with thee some of the folk that are with me. And he said, What needeth it? let me find grace in the sight of my lord.

¹⁶So Esau returned that day on his way unto Seir.

> ¹⁷And Jacob journeyed to Succoth, and built him an house, and made booths for his cattle: therefore the name of the place is called Succoth. ¹⁸And Jacob came to Shalem, a city of Shechem, which is in the land of Canaan, when he came from Padanaram; and pitched his tent before the city. (Gen. 33.1-18)

This must have been the most beautiful as well as the most bewildering scene to behold. The four hundred men with Esau knew he had every reason in the world to avenge the wrong done to him, and that he finally had the opportunity to settle the score with his brother. Without a doubt, those men were expecting to bathe their swords in the blood of Jacob and his family. How often did they witness their friend lamenting the anguish that gripped his soul, and expressing the rage that consumed his mind when he thought of his brother's deception? The anticipation of the moment—the pleasure they would share—when they would see the fear and dread on Jacob's face as Esau raised his sword to strike him down. The time had finally arrived. On this day, Esau would satisfy his lust for revenge.

However, to the astonishment of all, the narrator directs their hearts away from the anticipation of impending violence, bloodshed, and revenge. In contrast, he relates one of the most astonishing examples of the mighty work of *God*—the conversion of one's heart. For the grace and Spirit of *God* supernaturally replaced Esau's anger, hatred, and bitterness, with forgiveness and clemency. He was able to look at Jacob as the brother he loved, instead of the man he hated. The work of Reconciliation had begun!

The fearsome four hundred halted their advance, perhaps at the sight of Jacob approaching and bowing in obeisance seven times. Esau dismounted, left behind the weapons he could have used to inflict suffering and death, and ran toward his brother. Was he going to kill him with his bare hands? The men watched in utter bewilderment as the two embraced and hugged each other with tears of great joy and exhilaration. What an awesome testimony indeed! We can only wonder how much influence Isaac had on his son as he taught him the ways of the Lord—the ways of mercy, forgiveness, brotherly love, and unity. *God* had testified earlier that **he knew** Abraham would teach his sons the ways of the Lord, and it was quite apparent that he fulfilled a great service to *God* and his sons.

The point I want to re-emphasize here—with the eyes of four hundred men upon him—Esau **chose** to leave his weapons behind, abandon his lust for revenge, and thrust aside his determination to kill his brother. He had already agreed in his heart to submit to the teachings of his father who taught him the word and the attributes of the Living *God* he loved, devoted his life to, and trusted. He could have taken the path of Cain and killed his brother; but instead, he executed the will of *God*: to be merciful and forgiving. This was only the first step to reconciliation. They still had to learn to live in harmony with one another. After their reunion, the narrator leads us to believe that Jacob dwelt in the land for many years, side by side with Esau in peace.

With this story, *God* gave us an exemplary model we can emulate to initiate an enduring peace between the Palestinians and Israelis. Can we admit the Israelis have given the Palestinians reason to hate? Yes. Can we affirm that the Palestinians have determined in their hearts to exact revenge on their brothers? Yes. Can millions of people empathize with the Palestinians and understand the reasoning behind their malice and bitterness? No doubt. Will the execution of revenge bring about peace? Never.

I omitted a segment of this story unintentionally, but it seems appropriate to bring attention to it here. The story actually began with Rebekah asking the Lord about some difficulties she was having in her pregnancy. *God's* response was, *"Two nations are in thy womb, and two manner of people shall be separated from thy bowels; and <u>the one people shall be stronger</u> than the other people; and <u>the elder shall serve the younger</u>."* (Gen. 25.23)

Jacob was the younger; Esau was the elder, but which one was the stronger? How do we determine that one nation is stronger than another—by a show of muscular strength, military superiority, or population growth? None of these confirms superior strength. One wins today only to lose another day when his vulnerability is exposed.

As an example, do we admire the man that has a Herculean physique and the physical strength of Samson when we observe his reluctance to face a challenger? The proof of strength is in one's resoluteness to his convictions, particularly in times where in utter silence he demonstrates that his inner strength and faith is unshakeable. He is the one who can stand before multitudes suffering humiliation, shame, and defeat; yet, maintains the stamina and fortitude to trust in the teachings of his *God,* display *his* integrity, faith, honor, and inner confidence. He has the strength to stand tall, unwavering, steadfast, refusing to submit to the forces that demands he forsake the Rock of his faith, or face death. For even in the face of death, he wears the armor of his *God* with boldness and grace. He may not have the physique of a Hercules, but who can deny his superior strength?

Consider the parallels in the story: the Israelites gave their brother valid reasons throughout the centuries to abhor them and plan their annihilation. The Israelis have made overtures to appease their brother's anger and ill will by offering to share *their* land, abundance, and wealth—all to no avail. Like Jacob, the Israelis have returned to the land of their fathers after a long separation; but, unlike their father Jacob, they took an aggressive position, claimed the land as *their exclusive territory,* forced many to leave their homes, and provoked a conflict we still witness today. Am I taking sides with this statement? Not at all, for we must remember that Israel was also a victim of deception, and like the Palestinians, struggled to retrieve what they were convinced belonged to them alone. A peace initiative cannot be successfully implemented until Israel and the Palestinians acknowledge the Covenant *God* made with their father Abraham, in which *he* gave the land to "all" of his seed.

## THE SOLUTION to Peace in the Middle East

Like Esau, the Palestinians have the power in their hands to advance this initiative or reject it. It takes two willing parties to reconcile. The Palestinians can take the lead by following the example given in this story, setting aside their determination for vengeance, refusing to allow anger, revulsion and hatred for their brother to fill their hearts with murder, and replacing them with the *Godly* virtues of forgiveness and clemency. The sword is in their hand; and they can prove their strength and courage by making a heroic decision to set aside their weapons and embrace their brothers in peace. It is also in their power to reject peace and subject millions to needless bloodshed. While it takes some courage and skill to fight, it takes much greater courage to make peace. Turning the other cheek is not a sign of weakness, but of strength. If they choose to lift up the sword, there will be no winners. Their women need their husbands and the children need their fathers—living heroes, not dead martyrs. When Israelis and Palestinians look at their wives and children they should be able to say in their hearts, "Let us come together and pave the way for our families to live in peace."

Here is the irony of the situation: If the brothers do it *God's* way there will be no winners, but there will not be any losers, either. However, if they do it their way, (I am referring to rejecting peace) there will be no winners; instead, every family will suffer loss.

Esau had the eyes of four hundred men upon him; the Palestinians have the eyes of more than five billion on them. **Is there a better way to gain the admiration and respect of the entire world, become a modern example** of the power of ***God's*** **grace, and bring honor and glory to *God* and a deep respect for their father's legacy?** They will relish in victory when they succeed in fulfilling their goals. Finally, people throughout the world will acknowledge them as the honorable sons of Abraham, instead of Muslim extremists. What a great testimony of faith to the unbelievers as they witness the mighty work of *God* as the Palestinians and Israelis commit themselves to the conditions the Almighty God of Abraham would have them observe and practice; and acknowledge their "standing" to claim their inheritance.

Israel has the weaponry and military strength of Hercules; but their military superiority has not given them the ultimate victory—peace. It never will. So, who is the stronger brother—the Palestinians? Like the four hundred, we are the spectators. Will we see Jacob's blood spilled on the ground? Or, will we stand in awe as they display their inner strength and win the ultimate prize—peace?

## *THE HOLY SEED*

Truth is the ultimate peacemaker, but we can only realize its full potential when we are completely honest and willing to put aside our hostilities and rise above the enmity that grips our souls. The Israelis and Palestinians have similar concerns every mediator has ignored, minimized, or denied over the years, actions that were offensive to them. As stated several times already, in this conflict, two separate and distinct nations lay claim to being the "sole and rightful heir of their father Abraham's estate" including the right to receive, enjoy, and secure all real and personal property contained in the Covenant by divine decree. Is this the whole truth? I wish it were, but unfortunately, the dispute does not end here. As I said earlier, neither son can justify this claim. Ishmael, and Israel, are co-heirs of the land of Canaan, and named by God as the Holy Seed of Abraham. However, there are many descendants of Abraham alive today that only the Holy Father in Heaven can identify.

Remember, *God* told Abraham that he would be the **father of many nations** and that *he* would cause all nations to be blessed in him. So, does that mean there are others who may also be entitled to a portion of the inheritance? It would certainly appear to be a likely possibility. Let us, once again, recall the words of the Lord to Abraham:

> [4]As for me, this is my covenant with you: **You will be the father of many nations.**
> [5]No longer will you be called Abram ; your name will be Abraham, for **I have made you a father of many nations.**

> ⁶I will make you very fruitful; **I will make nations of you,** and **kings will come from you.**
> ⁷**I will establish my covenant as an everlasting covenant between me and you and your descendants after you for the generations to come, <u>to be your God and the God of your descendants after you.</u>**
> ⁸**The whole land of Canaan**, where you are now an alien, **I will give as an everlasting possession to you and your descendants after you; <u>and I will be their God.</u>** (Gen.17.4 -8 NIV emphasis added)

The Covenant identifies the **offspring** of Abraham as the "Rightful heirs to the land of Canaan." *ONE* may argue that the *Seed* who have established other nations are entitled to the lands they have founded, not Canaan. However, *ONE* would need to prove his argument. From the data I have examined, *God* never made that distinction. *He* told Abraham he would become the father of many nations, though *he* chose not to name any of them.

Can we imagine four to five billion people trying to take up residence within the borders of Palestine? I do not think so. However, if the Palestinians and Israelis agree on a peace accord, I can certainly imagine billions of people making a pilgrimage to the Holy Land to worship Almighty *God*. I can also see the economies of the Israelis and Palestinians bursting with prosperity. ***Canaan was the original homeland***—the promised inheritance—***not the only land*** his children were to set up and inhabit. However, in order for us to grasp this truth, we must be introduced to *God's* original plan and be able to identify *his* wisdom and recognize the love *he* has for us. As *he* spoke through the prophet Jeremiah: **"For I know the plans I have for you," declares the LORD, "plans to prosper you and not to harm you, plans to give you hope and a future**. Then you will call upon me and come and pray to me, and I will listen to you. You will seek me and find me when you seek me with all your heart." (Jer. 29:11-13 NIV emphasis added)

It has always been *God's* will to have One Seed, One Tree of Life, rooted and grounded in the love of *God*, One Family, with many strong branches bearing the fruits of righteousness and faith—ultimately One Kingdom, ruled by One King—the Lord Almighty. To accomplish this, *he* set the following plan in motion:

*He* planted *his family* in the land of Canaan and confirmed Abraham as its founding father. From Canaan, *God* said he would increase Abraham's seed to exceedingly vast numbers, compelling them to expand their borders from generation to generation, until the entire earth was occupied with Abraham's seed. This was the plan *God* was referring to when *he* told Abraham to count the stars if he was able, because his seed would be that numerous. When the plan of worldwide expansion was accomplished, *God's* promise that Abraham would become the father of many nations, and that *all the earth* would be blessed in him, would be fulfilled; and, of course, our *God* would reign as Lord and King over all the earth. This was, is, and forever will be—*God's* plan!

The liberals and unbelievers make a mockery of *God*'s plan, calling it *Utopian and Impossible* to fulfill. What they fail to realize is the *God* of wisdom is incapable of devising a plan that is impossible to accomplish.

There are serious questions that deserve an answer from the enlightened ones, namely: If this was truly *God's* plan, why were none of Abraham's seed taught to honor *God* by submitting themselves to the fulfillment of *his* will? Instead of waging war with our brothers and killing one another, we could have been engaged in heart-warming competitions to see which of us *God* would multiply the fastest, and which one would establish the greater number of nations? Moreover, once we populated the entire earth, we would have no enemies, and our *God*, and our Father's *God* would reign over all the earth and we would be *his* servants living in everlasting peace, prosperity, and joy! Why was *his* plan hidden from our eyes?

Remember, The Adversary planned to rule the earth, so he set up his pawns, had them distort the words and the will of *God*, and established his "leaders" to guide the people in propaganda and lies; and increase their anger and hate for one another until the nations engaged in war. It was always his intent to conquer Jerusalem, the throne of the Lord, for himself, and cause all the earth to worship the beast instead of the Creator. This plan has been in motion for many, many centuries, and the brothers were not his only victims. I will discuss more on Jerusalem later.

This is one instance where I am able to expose the reality of *God*, and the essence of *his truth*. Compare the similarity between these two statements: 1) **God's plan, (*what many believe*), provided for the establishment of <u>one religion</u>, <u>one race</u>, <u>one nationality</u>, and <u>one culture</u>.** (This would be an example of the identical twin I spoke of earlier.)

2) ***God's* plan, (*his truth*), provided for the perpetuation of <u>one family</u> joined in heart and spirit; <u>one nation</u> of many peoples, having <u>one identity</u>, <u>joint heirs, and co-citizens</u> of God's Kingdom, sharing the inheritance of their father, and benefitting from the presence and blessings of God—the rewards of their love, respect, and devotion to him, and the free exercise of their charity, (love) one towards the other.**

This is the difference between religious doctrine everyone must "*accept by faith*" because there are Scripture verses that give some "factual credibility" to them, and *Godly truth*. Truth expresses the faithfulness of *his* grace and mercy when he is accepting of us, an imperfect people who, despite our failings, devote ourselves to loving *him*, and declare our loyalty and faith to *him* as the only true *God*, and the *God* of our father, Abraham. Truth exposes *his* willingness to bless us and to share in the fulfillment of *his* love. Truth enables us to visualize his joys and delights in seeing his children happy, free, and secure!

As we look back at the two statements of "faith", in the highlights above, which one illuminates the nature of a *God* of love, grace, mercy, and everlasting righteousness? In addition, which one would lead people to believe that *God* is prejudiced, biased, and discriminatory? Which one would make us ask, "Why did you bring me into this world, and allow me to be born to a ---------- who is not of the One true race and culture?" You may say, "Who can question *God*?" I have a hard time picturing myself, or anyone else for that matter, standing before the Judge of all the earth, being denied entrance into his kingdom, simply because I did not meet the specifications of race, culture, nationality or religion; and not question his "righteous judgment." Jesus of Nazareth gave us an interesting lesson concerning that day. He said,

> [32]All the nations will be gathered before him, and **he will separate the people one from another as a shepherd separates the sheep from the goats.**
> [33]**He will put the sheep on his right and the goats on his left.**
> [34]Then the King will say to those on his right, 'Come, you who are blessed by my Father; take your inheritance, the kingdom prepared for you since the creation of the world.
> [35]*For I was hungry and you gave me something to eat, I was thirsty and you gave me something to drink, I was a stranger and you invited me in,*
> [36] *I needed clothes and you clothed me, I was sick and you looked after me, I was in prison and you came to visit me.'*
> [37]Then the righteous will answer him, **'Lord, when did we see you hungry and feed you, or thirsty and give you something to drink?**
> [38]**When did we see you a stranger and invite you in, or needing clothes and clothe you?**

**³⁹When did we see you sick or in prison and go to visit you?'**
⁴⁰The King will reply, 'I tell you the truth, whatever you did for one of the least of these brothers of mine, you did for me.'
⁴¹Then he will say to those on his left, *'Depart from me, you who are cursed, into the eternal fire prepared for the devil and his angels.*
⁴²*For I was hungry and you gave me nothing to eat, I was thirsty and you gave me nothing to drink,*
⁴³*I was a stranger and you did not invite me in, I needed clothes and you did not clothe me, I was sick and in prison and you did not look after me.'*
⁴⁴**They also will answer, 'Lord, when did we see you hungry or thirsty or a stranger or needing clothes or sick or in prison, and did not help you?'**
⁴⁵He will reply, 'I tell you the truth, whatever you did not do for one of the least of these, you did not do for me.'
⁴⁶Then they will go away to eternal punishment, but the righteous to eternal life. (Matt.25:32-46 NIV)

**(Take note: not only the accursed, but also the righteous will question the Lord's judgment on that day.)** I cannot imagine questioning the Lord's decision when *he is welcoming me into his kingdom.* All I can think of, it must be one of those imperfections imbedded in our human nature. Fortunately, there is no mention of race, nationality, religion, or culture. The only virtue mentioned is the charitable work of *Godly* righteousness—putting the needs, cares, and concerns of the needy before one self.

Who among us has the wisdom to identify the *"**The Holy Seed**"* today, particularly those with diverse national origins? The fact is, only Our Heavenly Father can make a positive identification of *his* children; and *he* will surely separate the chaff from the wheat, the good seed from the bad. Man looks at the outer appearance, his genealogical background, the land of his origin, etc; but *God* simply looks upon the heart, the soul, the part no man can see, to identify *his* own.

Take Moses for an example. In his days, most of the Israelites only knew that Moses was the son of Pharaoh, an obvious pagan and idol worshipper. We do not have any idea what his reputation was, or know how he treated the slaves. Undoubtedly, the word spread quickly among them that Moses killed a fellow Egyptian and ran away to escape the judgment of Pharaoh. If these perceptions were all the Israelites had to go on, I can only wonder how many of them could have been convinced that Moses was truly a child of *God*, of the seed of Abraham, and called by the *God* of Abraham to be a prophet? I would doubt anyone beyond his immediate family.

*God* knows those who are *his*. *He* made allowance for the forty years Moses worshipped idols. After all, *he* was the *one* who saved Moses' life by having Pharaoh's daughter discover him in the reeds. By virtue of *his* grace, *he* revealed *his* identity to Moses; separated him from that life; confirmed *hi*s identity to him, and ultimately called him to deliver the Seed of Abraham out of Egypt. This story, if no other, opens our eyes to the reality that many people of Abraham's lineage may be born and raised in countries and cultures where our identity is unknown, even to ourselves.

Consider the benefit imputed to us, by virtue of Abraham's life of faith and devotion to the Living *God* in the integrity of his heart; a life *God* found pleasing, and *who* adorned him with a mantle of righteousness that *he* passed on to his seed. Whether we are Caucasian, Middle Eastern, Asian, African, or one of many other races, we, the seed of Abraham, have this "braided covering" imputed to us because of our devotion and faith to Abraham's *God*.

By means of Abraham's covering, we are endowed with the *Godly* virtues of hospitality, integrity, justice, and morality. The Almighty *God, himself,* imputes it to those of us who love peace and harmony, who would only engage in warfare to protect our land and families, who believe in advancing the virtues of righteousness, and practice the beauty of charity, (making allowances for another's lack of knowledge, skill, or sufficiency). We give from our hearts; considering the next one we have opportunity to help may be an angel of the Lord. We are a people who desire *God's* blessings, conceding with a repentant heart that as hard as we try, we fail *him* every day; that we are imperfect and undeserving of the least of his mercies and grace. *God* is the primary object of our affection, the *One* we serve willingly, not just as an act of obedience to compulsory mandates and religious dogmas, but out of devotion and love for the *One* who redeemed us by *his* grace. It may be this covering or mantle of righteousness that allows the angels to separate the sheep from the goats on that day. All

I am certain of is this; according to the text, when the King takes notice of our virtues, *he* welcomes us into *his* kingdom.

Consider the truth I am imparting to you in the next few sentences. *God* never shackled our father, Abraham, his sons, and their extended family, with mandates on how to worship *him*. *He* wanted Abraham's worship, love, and devotion to come from a sincere heart and an upright spirit, not from a directive to fulfill some religious obligation. *God* is truth; and *he* wants us to worship *him* in spirit, and in truth. Does a man or woman want us to show our love to them because we feel that we have a duty, an obligation to perform; or because our hearts are filled with such love and devotion, we want to please them and make them happy? Who would want less in a relationship? Does *God* deserve less?

May we conclude then that everyone who lives a moral life is a descendant of Abraham? No, of course not; but then again, who among us has the spiritual discernment to make the distinction without prejudice? There is no one, except for *God,* capable of separating the true sheep from the wolves in sheep's clothing. Man corrupts himself by his absolute disregard, rejection, and utter contempt for *God, his* plan, *his* people, and *his* word. This is what condemns him, and brings a curse upon his family, community, and country. Jesus of Nazareth addressed his followers with this question and answer: "Do not ye yet understand, that whatsoever entereth in at the mouth goeth into the belly, and is cast out into the draught? But those things which proceed out of the mouth come forth from the heart; and they defile the man. For out of the heart proceed evil thoughts, murders, adulteries, fornications, thefts, false witness, blasphemies: These are the things which defile a man: but to eat with unwashen hands defileth not a man. (Mt. 15.17-20)

I realize that I am being repetitive but the Lord is well known for repeating precepts worth memorizing. The Holy Seed is comprised of many nationalities and creeds scattered throughout the world; we are the Holy Children of *God* Almighty; and, only *he* can certify those who are *his*; and *he* is the only *one* entitled to exercise that right. Which one of us would appreciate someone telling our sons or our daughters they are not our children; or, that we are not their parents because they do not see the resemblance? Yet, we know the child is ours. Undoubtedly, we would ask this one question of them, "What gives you the right to decide who is a member of our family?"

This book is not an encouragement to any group to take aggressive action to bring down their government. That is not the message, nor is it the way. Before the Israelites left Egypt, did *God* command them to overthrow Pharaoh's government? If its overthrow was necessary, *God* showed them *he* was able to do it without their help. What did *God* ask the people to do? *He* told them to cleanse their hearts, forgive one another, and come together with one voice in prayer to the One *God*. *He* would take care of the rest.

*"Two nations are in thy womb, and two manner of people shall be separated from thy bowels; and the one people shall be stronger than the other people; and the elder shall serve the younger."* (Gen. 25.23)

Esau and Ishmael would be identified with the Arab population while Jacob would become the Israelite nation. Both sons have had their conflicts and troubles in this life. Was it God's intention they suffer such maladies because they were sinners in his sight? No. John, the disciple of Jesus related this incident: "As he (Jesus) went along, he saw a man blind from birth. His disciples asked him, 'Rabbi, who sinned, this man or his parents, that he was born blind?' 'Neither this man nor his parents sinned,' said Jesus, 'but this happened so that the work of God might be displayed in his life.'"

Saul of Tarsus, a learned rabbi, and convert to Christianity said this in regards to Israel: "For I would not, brethren, that ye should be ignorant of this mystery, lest ye should be wise in your own conceits; that blindness in part is happened to Israel, until the fullness of the Gentiles be come in. And so all Israel shall be saved...." (Rom. 11. 25, 26)

This is the word of the Lord, "Israelis and Palestinians have been blinded to the truths that would have benefitted them in the flesh. However, because of their blindness, multitudes have been able to see. Now it is time that your eyes should be opened, that you may see, and be a witness to the mercies of *God,* and reap the rewards for your suffering." And, "The LORD hath heard thy affliction, O' Ishmael."

We must break up the fallow ground, the weakened foundation of our faith undermined by bitterness, lies, and deception, begin to lay the groundwork for a working and lasting peace void of prejudice, hatred, and political power grabbing. Let those of us who desire peace and unity begin to come together with one another in prayer with the primary goal of re-establishing our identity in the same spirit as Abraham. If the liberals and power grabbers are against this, so be it. As the Holy Seed gathers in *his* name and yields to *his* Holy Spirit, we will begin to witness *his* mighty hand at work. We will be part of *his* plan and witnesses to its fulfillment. Those of us endowed with a deep inner faith, determination, and conviction in the Almighty *God* of Abraham must lead the way.

The strength of our faith—is found in our works of charity, love, and forgiveness—virtues that spring to life from an inner faith, an upright heart, even the same faith Abraham practiced and found favor with God? The true and living *God* of Abraham will not judge us by **the faith we profess**; but by our deeds that please *him*, the expression of the **faith we possess.** This is the faith that seals our identities, allows us to recognize one another as a fellow citizen of the household of faith; and a member of The Holy Seed, a Child of Abraham, whether we call ourselves Muslims, Jews, or Christians. These are the people we dare not deny, but embrace, care for, work with, and be a vessel of honor unto the Lord our *God;* a vessel *he* is able to use to set the captives free, provide a perpetual inheritance, establish *his* kingdom, and fulfill *his* eternal plan.

Palestinians, you have the opportunity to change the way you are currently perceived, to a people of conviction and faith, strong enough to stretch out your hand in peace, and weak enough to cry with, and minister to, those who are suffering.

**Remember…On that day…you will say…**

'Lord, when did we see you hungry and feed you, or thirsty and give you something to drink? When did we see you a stranger and invite you in, or needing clothes and clothe you? When did we see you sick or in prison and go to visit you?'

"The King will reply, 'I tell you the truth, whatever you did for one of the least of these brothers of mine, you did for me.'"

# *LAYING THE GROUNDWORK FOR PEACE*

## º **FORMATION OF A NATIONAL GOVERNMENT**

Palestinians seek a separate state that will enable self-governance. This is a well-recognized fact. However, I believe Truth reveals desires and ambitions a one-state solution would best provide for—Justice, Security, and Peace.

There are two main "solutions" on the table that I am aware of, a one state solution, and a two state solution. While I am not privy to all the intricacies of the plans, I am inclined to believe the one-state solution presents the best option for success. First of all, one-state (country) comprised of many diverse ideologies and cultures demonstrating their ability to form a coalition based on mutual respect and concern for the security and economic success of the nation as a whole presents a formidable position of strength to the entire world. On the other hand, a two state solution would present a weaker position internationally. Competing nations would surely attempt to draw one of the two states into an alliance the other may perceive as a potential threat; and once again, peace would be short lived. Secondly, negotiations for justice, security, defense, natural resources, individual rights, free enterprise, and a host of other issues, may be decided, <u>if at all</u>, after many needless delays and political posturing. Thirdly, it would not close the gap of suspicion and resentment that would continue to exist between the peoples. In short, a two-state solution leaves too many holes to plug. Moreover, how do we justify the concept that a two-state solution is compatible with *God's* original plan for one nation and kingdom? Justice is the Power that enforces the Golden Rule, the Divine decree that commands the people to use their privileges, property, and rights, in ways that prevent harm or injury to another and to treat others in the same way they would want to be treated.

Peace and security must be the ultimate goal. For more than six decades, various political ambassadors have tried to broker a peace agreement to no avail. True peace can only become a reality when *all the people* share goals, statutes of law and justice void of bias or prejudice. Both families want peace; but peace cannot be achieved as long as well-meaning negotiators fail to identify, or fail to satisfy, the issues of vital importance to the parties. Peace cannot exist where the nation is in a constant state of chaos, suspicion, or threatening hostilities; neither can a people dwell together in peace where one segment of their society appears to be enjoying more opportunities and privileges than the other. Unrest breeds distrust, and distrust leads to rebellion and conflict. Israelis and Palestinians must agree to set aside all rhetoric and threats of war for the sake of *God*, family, children, and country; and begin a dialogue that will result in the equitable distribution of law, justice, and security for everyone in the land.

To sustain peace among the brothers, it is essential that all Palestinians, Israelis, and Christians respect the value and dedication each holds for their religious worship. To the sincere in heart, the worship of *God* is not a mere practice of religion, but a dominant and inclusive force in their lives that stabilizes and preserves the moral fiber of their families and communities.

The *"Seed of Abraham"* should be permitted to practice our faith and cultural traditions without outside interference or persecution within our communities and worship centers. We believe in One *God*, One Savior, and One Lord over all. I say this because faithful Jews, Muslims, and Christians identify with, and ultimately worship, the *God* of Abraham, as did the founders of these particular faiths, Mohammed, Moses, and Jesus of Nazareth. Moreover, as was stated earlier in this book, just because we call someone by a different name does not alter his nature or change his appearance. The same is true for the Living *God*.

At the appointed time, known only to our Father in Heaven, the Lord will cause everyone to know *his* identity; and *he* will not require the help of any one of us to bring it to pass. The prophet Jeremiah declared that everyone would know, not simply believe, who *he* is. He said, *"And they shall teach no more every man his neighbor, and every man his brother, saying, Know the LORD: for they shall all know me, from the least of them unto the greatest of them, saith the LORD: for I will forgive their iniquity, and I will remember their sin no more."* (Jer. 31.34 KJV)

*God* is Love: the enriched essence of truth, fullness of happiness, and blessings. Although *God* is invisible, his presence and Love is discernible in *his* works of charity, forgiveness, strong faith, reconciliation, justice and equity, patience, kindness, setting aside all hostilities and threats, and embracing the righteousness of *God* found in peace and integrity. Love is the solid rock, the sustainable foundation of Hope and Freedom, upon which the descendants of Abraham can build a secure future for their posterity.

## ° SECURITY

In the Land of Promise, Israelis and Palestinians alike must be able to provide the means to secure their families against unwanted dangers that arise from all threats, foreign and domestic. The answer is not in building walls of separation between two peace-loving people, but in separating those whose hearts are set on malice. Foreign leaders and propagandists will witness a decrease in their influence as the people come together in unity. Beware of them.

The Holy Land is no place for hiding assassins and conspirators who are intent on terrorizing, controlling, and destroying innocent lives in order to satisfy their own lusts. Security must be the highest priority. People should expect from their leadership nothing less than what a wife and children should expect from a good husband and father. Above all other needs, including food and water, he must provide for their security.

Conspiracy theorists have promoted the view that certain powerful members of highly secretive groups and societies have conceived a master plan for the formation of a one-world government order. Is it true? I have my views but I do not have any substantial proof readily available. They claim the intent of the schemers is to bankrupt every economy and force all nations to adopt one currency and one governmental authority. It is certainly plausible if we consider how many economies are in financial distress. If it is true, do we act as if they will give Palestinians, Israelis, and others a special exemption in this worldwide scheme of things? If the brothers take heed to the teachings of the Lord our *God*, particularly those having to do with charity, the *Promised Land* will become the most powerful nation on earth, economically, militarily, and spiritually. The nations will borrow from you, but you will have no need to borrow from them. They will fear you, but you will have no reason to fear them.

º **ISSUES OF GRAVE IMPORTANCE**

• In order to minimize the chances of animosity and hostility, every citizen must have equal opportunity to <u>Prosper,</u> including the right to <u>Unrestricted Freedom of Movement</u>. Talking and believing accomplishes nothing where there is no visible effort being shown.

• Here is an issue of conscience: If the brothers reach a consensus on the Covenant, and agree that it is inclusive of all the righteous seed of Abraham, then by what authority do we prevent one or more from acquiring their portion? I am referring, in particular, to those who have been deprived of their homeland, whether Jew or Muslim who wish to return to their inheritance. This is only fair and reasonable.

• There are certain unalienable rights that do not require the approval of any government or nation to be exercised. Among these are the Right to Life, Liberty, and the Pursuit of Happiness, Employment without prejudice or bias, a <u>Quality Education</u> for all children, <u>Equal Housing Opportunities</u> unrestricted by race or creed, the <u>Right to Compete in local and international Commerce and Trade</u>

Markets, and Equal Justice for all are but a few of the benefits that are assimilated in this bundle of unalienable rights. A people who enjoy these freedoms are a blessed people indeed; and contentment is the sister of peace.

• As I stated previously, many will attempt to make strong arguments that the land should be occupied by those whose bloodline descends from Abraham whether they live righteously or not. Let them be. These have no regard for the Bible or Qur'an, which teach otherwise. Do not be overly concerned: *God* will separate *his* children from the wicked.

As their leaders begin to share the good news they have reached a mutual agreement for peace, the people will probably reserve any display of joyfulness until they hear the verdict on the future of Jerusalem.

## *JERUSALEM*

The Seed of Abraham should be aware that *God* never intended for Jerusalem to be the capital city of the Jews, Muslims, Christians, or any other religious or ethnic group; nor, did *he* intend for it to become an "international city" controlled by foreign interests. The Holy City of Jerusalem, not the Vatican in Rome, was predestined to be the *Holy City of God*, the symbolic place of *his* throne, and the center of worship open to all peoples on earth, as declared by the prophets:

> $^{23}$In that day shall there be a highway out of Egypt to Assyria, and the Assyrian shall come into Egypt, and the Egyptian into Assyria, and the Egyptians shall serve with the Assyrians.
> $^{24}$In that day shall Israel be the third with Egypt and with Assyria, even a blessing in the midst of the land:
> $^{25}$Whom the LORD of hosts shall bless, saying, **Blessed be Egypt my people**, and **Assyria the work of my hands**, and **Israel mine inheritance.** (Isa 19:23-25 emphasis added)

> At that time **they shall call Jerusalem the throne of the LORD;** and all the nations shall be gathered unto it, to the name of the LORD, to Jerusalem: neither shall they walk any more after the imagination of their evil heart.
> (Jer. 3.17 emphasis added)

³Thus saith the LORD; I am returned unto Zion, and will dwell in the midst of Jerusalem: and **Jerusalem shall be called a city of truth; and the mountain of the LORD of hosts the holy mountain.**
⁴Thus saith the LORD of hosts; There shall yet old men and old women dwell in the streets of Jerusalem, and every man with his staff in his hand for very age.
⁵ And the streets of the city shall be full of boys and girls playing in the streets thereof.
⁶Thus saith the LORD of hosts; If it be marvellous in the eyes of the remnant of this people in these days, should it also be marvellous in mine eyes? saith the LORD of hosts.
⁷Thus saith the LORD of hosts; Behold, I will save my people from the east country, and from the west country;
⁸**And I will bring them, and they shall dwell in the midst of Jerusalem: and they shall be my people, and I will be their *God*, in truth and in righteousness.**
⁹Thus saith the LORD of hosts; Let your hands be strong, ye that hear in these days these words by the mouth of the prophets, which were in the day that the foundation of the house of the LORD of hosts was laid, that the temple might be built. (Zech. 8.3–9 emphasis added)

Therefore, on that blessed day let the leaders and clergy gather the seed of Abraham together and announce these decrees are to be written, ordered, and executed on behalf of all the seed of Abraham!

- The seed of Abraham hereby tithes, offers, grants, conveys, dedicates, and consecrates the holy mountain on which Jerusalem is built unto the *God of Abraham*.

- The seed of Abraham forbids any nation on earth from claiming Jerusalem as its capital city, now or in the future; that it shall be known throughout the world as the **City of God**, **the Holy Mountain of God**, **The Holy City**, **the City of Truth**, and the **Throne of the Lord**.

- Let the glorious houses of worship and prayer be built to the honor and glory of **Our Heavenly Father**, known to us and worshipped as the ***God* of Abraham,** and the **Almighty God.**

- Let all the seed of Abraham forever esteem Jerusalem and Mount Zion as a Most Holy place where all people on earth may come and freely worship the *God of Heaven* – according to their own faith and preference without fear or intimidation.

To summarize, if both parties are willing to make peace by way of the "Covenant of Promise", the probability of war engulfing the region is extremely low. However, if they are not willing, war is inevitable; a war where there will be no declared winners. We may call them martyrs, soldiers, terrorists, liberators, or some other name, but there is only one common name for them all—*Dead Heroes*; and their mothers and loved ones, "the Mourners."

Reconciliation is definitely within reach; and once confirmed, will result in an outpouring of great blessings and economic abundance for all the seed of Abraham. The news of peace in the Holy Land will prompt an immediate ripple effect worldwide. People of every nation will join in the celebration of victory—not of war—but of peace; and they will visit the land without fear to worship the *God of Heaven* according to their own faiths. The merchants will dance in the streets; Arabs, Israelis, and Christians alike will enjoy prosperity as never before. Instead of spending billions in weaponry, the nation can rebuild its economy and restore affluence to their people as it was prophesied, *"And they shall beat their swords into plowshares, and their spears into pruning hooks: nation shall not lift up sword against nation, neither shall they learn war any more."* (Isa.2.4)

The streets will burst forth in ecstatic joy and merriment. All who claim Abraham to be their father will reconcile and celebrate the delights of peace and freedom. There will be even greater jubilation knowing that the *God* of Abraham has visited them—the proofs of which are the changes that took place in their hearts. What an awesome *God* who replaces bitterness and hatred with forgiveness and acceptance—and the reality of being in accord with *his* divine will. *God* has given us the opportunity to bring this dream to fruition—the opportunity to dedicate the Holy Mountain in Jerusalem to the Living *God*. Plus, *he* has prepared the way for the construction of the most renowned houses of worship on earth, and the opportunity to reinstitute the plan *he* put in place when *he* took our father, Abraham, from his country and brought him to the land of Canaan. Let us pledge to unite in harmony and allow *him* to complete *his* plan to establish One Family, One Holy Nation, over whom *Our God*, the Almighty *God* of our father, Abraham, will reign as Lord and King forever. Is *he* not worthy?

Is this the word of *God?* Do not accept it by faith, and do not deny it because your beliefs differ from what is written herein. Make every attempt at proving the essence of *God*, *his* will, *his* work, and *his* truth, not looking for issues to debate. If you ask the Lord to confirm *his* word, he *will*. And, you will see the evidence of Truth, as the work of reconciliation will not only begin, but will succeed. *God's* presence will be manifested by a calm peace that will begin to settle upon the nation, (your enemies will be at peace with you), and the Spirit of Unity will be at work overcoming vanity and replacing the evils of pride and hostility.

Let us unite in committing our hearts and lives to the Lord as Joshua the prophet did when he declared before the people these words;

**"AS FOR ME AND MY HOUSE, WE WILL SERVE THE LORD."**

Let it be accomplished, O Lord, for the majestic splendor of your holiness and mercy. Amen.

www.ingramcontent.com/pod-product-compliance
Lightning Source LLC
Chambersburg PA
CBHW071512040426
42444CB00008B/1605